Vancouver Seattle Victoria

**A POCKET GUIDE
TO THE EVERGREEN
TRIANGLE**

ARCHIE SATTERFIELD

GREY*S*TONE BOOKS
Douglas & McIntyre
Vancouver / Toronto

Greystone Books
A division of Douglas & McIntyre, 1615 Venables Street
Vancouver, British Columbia V5L 2H1

Canadian Cataloguing in Publication Data
Satterfield, Archie
    Vancouver-Seattle-Victoria
    A Pocket Guide to the Evergreen Triangle

    ISBN 1-55054-101-3
1. Vancouver (B.C.) —Guidebooks.   2. Victoria (B.C.) —Guidebooks.
3. Seattle (Wash.) —Guidebooks.   4. British Columbia —Guidebooks.
5. Washington (State) —Guidebooks.
I. Title
FC3807.S27 1995   917.1104'4   C95-910012-1
F1087.S27 1995

Cover illustration by DesignGeist
Cover and text design by DesignGeist
Maps by Ed Walker
Printed and bound in Canada by Best Gagné Book Manufacturers, Inc.
Printed on acid-free paper ∞

The publisher gratefully acknowledges the assistance of the Canada
Council and of the British Columbia Ministry of Tourism, Small
Business and Culture for its publishing programs.

Extreme care has been taken to ensure that all information in this book
is accurate and up to date, but neither the author nor the publisher can
be held legally responsible for any errors that may appear.

CONTENTS

The Evergreen Triangle

Strait of Georgia

NEWCAS

Nanaimo

Ladysmith

Chema

Dun
Cowichan
Mill

*Vancouver
Island*

Strait of
Juan de Fuca

101

N

0   10
Miles

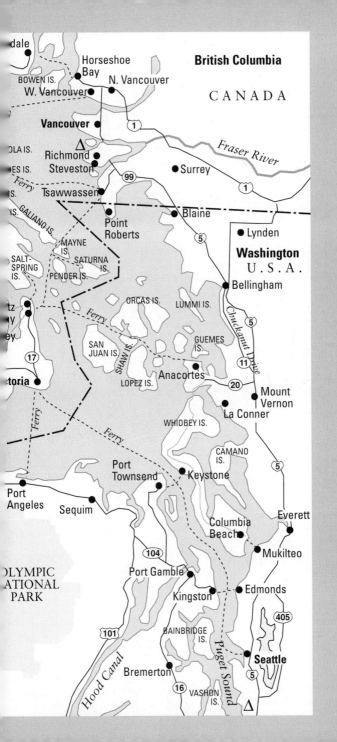

To Jerome Richard,
who gave me the idea for the book,
then suggested the title.
But when I asked him to write
it for me, he refused.

Introduction

This book came about when Sandra Katz from South Carolina, visiting my friends Jerome and Carolyn Richard, wondered why nobody had written a guide to all three cities. So did I and I took it as an opportunity to accomplish something I was unable to while working as an editor and book critic on Seattle newspapers: to treat the entire region as a whole rather than as two distinct countries.

The tourism industry sometimes promotes the region as the "Two Nation Vacation," and this is possible because few countries in the world are better neighbors than Canada and the United States. In spite of obvious national and cultural differences, few places along the transcontinental border are more alike than Vancouver, Victoria and Seattle. The three have the same climate and similar scenery, and all three are in a part of the continent that is perhaps best described as socially benign. In spite of a measurable decrease in common courtesy, I don't know of another part of North America where civility is more common. Since Canada is far more mild than the United States —I once read that Canada is a decaffeinated version of the U. S.—I don't think it would be stretching the imagination to say that Seattle is more Canadian than any other American city.

Hardly a visitor comes to one of the cities without seeing at least one of the other two, and often all three. Usually American tourists come to Seattle, rent a car and drive to Vancouver. Then they go by B.C. Ferry to Nanaimo on Vancouver Island via Horseshoe Bay in West Vancouver or take a ferry at Tsawwassen near the U.S. border bound for Swartz Bay near Victoria. Thousands of other Americans who go on a cruise through the Inside Passage to Alaska arrive in Seattle or Bellingham, take a motorcoach north to Vancouver and spend a day or two, then go down to the stunningly beautiful cruise-ship terminal at Canada Place on Vancouver's Coal Harbour and board their ship.

Many visitors to Seattle don't feel their visit is complete without a trip by boat to Victoria. For decades the preferred Slow Boat to Victoria was the venerable passenger ship *Princess Marguerite*. She has only recently been replaced by the Victoria Clipper catamarans that are much faster and more comfortable.

Other passenger ferries are going into service, not only between the three major cities but also among the San Juan and Gulf Islands and between them and the mainland. Before highways were built in the region, hundreds of passenger and freight boats made scheduled runs all along this waterway, and because they were so small and so busy, they were known as the Mosquito Fleet. History is repeating itself with the return of this fleet of small passenger boats.

I have organized the book with a south-to-north orientation only because many more visitors come to the Evergreen Triangle from the United States than from Canada, beginning their trip in Seattle. I hope this approach will not be misinterpreted as a bias. The triangle traffic generally flows in this manner:

From Seattle to Vancouver via the mainland and Whidbey Island; from Seattle to Victoria via the San Juan Islands; from Seattle to Victoria via Port Angeles; from Seattle and Vancouver to Victoria and the Gulf Islands via the ferry at Tsawwassen; from Victoria to Nanaimo, and across to Horseshoe Bay in Vancouver; from Vancouver via Horseshoe Bay to Nanaimo and on to Victoria.

During the past decade the world has beaten a path to the Evergreen Triangle. Seattle, Vancouver and Victoria have shown a steady growth with Vancouver's growth a bit faster due to the large influx of Hong Kong residents who have been moving to Vancouver ahead of the Chinese takeover of Hong Kong that will be official in 1997. The decline of the timber industry is giving tourism another boost as outlying small towns seek means of both surviving and thriving.

Attention has not been a problem for the area. If anything, the three cities are in danger of being loved to death. In the past few years you could hardly pick up a magazine or newspaper without reading that Seattle had been

selected America's most livable city, or the cleanest, or the best place to raise kids, the best place to ride a bicycle, the best place to shop. Because of its quick response to medical emergencies, it was even proclaimed the best place in America to have a heart attack.

In addition to its natural beauty and good urban planning, Vancouver is a major business center, and the Port of Vancouver is the largest dry cargo facility on the North American Pacific Coast. In fact, it is probably Canada's wealthiest city, and it continues to attract wealth from around the world.

Victoria's popularity with international tourists continues to grow and it remains a favored retirement area, particularly for provincial bureaucrats who come to Victoria to work and decide to remain after retirement, as well as

North Vancouver's Capilano ∧
Suspension Bridge, a popular attraction.
Tourism Vancouver

for a continuing number of retired couples from the United Kingdom. Victoria is an end-of-the-road kind of place, so the downtown district is not afflicted with the freeways and elevated expressways of Seattle. It does have heavy traffic, in part because of its role as the seat of the provincial government and in part because it is so dependent on tourism.

Combine these human-sized cities with the magnificent scenery of the region, the damp but congenial climate, the perpetual greenery that surrounds the lakes, the blue-and-green beauty of Puget Sound, the Strait of Juan de Fuca and the Strait of Georgia with the mountain ranges for a backdrop, and you can understand why people living in places without those amenities would be interested in at least visiting the region, if not moving there.

While researching this book, I quickly learned that residents enjoy the area as much as visitors. Once I declined a dinner invitation in Seattle because I had to go to Vancouver Island. I must have said it poorly because I was quickly reminded that nobody "has" to go there; people go there by conscious choice and feel privileged to do so.

A FEW THINGS YOU SHOULD KNOW

Sometimes Americans visiting Canada for the first time are disappointed that it doesn't look that much different from the United States: same cars, same clothing, many of the same fast-food chains, similar architecture. Even the people look much the same, although Canada does seem to have a richer or at least more visible racial and cultural mix.

The monetary system is also quite similar, and the exchange rate hovers around a ratio of one U.S. dollar to $1.20 Canadian. Both countries have pennies, nickels, dimes and quarters. Canada's smallest piece of currency is a two-dollar bill; it does not have a one-dollar bill. Instead Canada uses a dollar coin called the Loony because it features a portrait of a loon. It is irregularly shaped to make it easy to identify by feel. Other than the obvious differences in color and design, the paper currency is in the same denominations in both countries, except that the two-dollar bill is more common in Canada.

Most other differences are subtle, and it is possible to travel in either country for days or weeks without feeling in the least alien.

At the risk of irritating some readers, here are some basic differences I have found between the two countries. Americans are more image conscious than Canadians, and American women tend to wear more makeup. Canadians are much more aware of America than vice versa, and this is a source of irritation to Canadians, who follow American events and politics very closely. Most Americans cannot name all or even most of the Canadian provinces, and many Americans don't know the Canadian form of government. (It is the Parliamentary form, modeled on that of England, including the Senate, a controversial version of the House of Lords because its members are appointed for life.)

The streets of Vancouver and Victoria are much safer than those in Seattle. The incidence of crimes of violence all across Canada is so low that Americans should be ashamed. Seattle has a murder rate of about 60 per year, low by American standards but shameful when compared with Vancouver's 28 to 30 per year and Victoria's fewer than 10 per year.

All three cities are plagued by panhandlers. Street people tend to become more and more aggressive as their numbers increase, and the cities continually wrestle with the moral and legal questions surrounding the street people's rights to live somewhere, and the rights of employed citizens with homes to go about their lives without being badgered.

Service tends to be better in Washington than in British Columbia. This doesn't mean that clerks and food servers are rude in British Columbia; they aren't. They just aren't trained to anticipate. If you want something in Canada, you will probably have to ask for it, and if you are in a department store you may have to go in search of a clerk. Washington has a reputation for attentive service that goes back several generations, a tradition begun by the late, great Frederick & Nelson department store and refined by Nordstrom's department store chain. The emphasis on good service was picked up by hotels and restaurants and is one of Washington's strongest traditions.

This doesn't take into account some of my pet irritants: few merchants in Washington will accept Canadian currency, while American currency is almost never rejected in Canada. In Washington, too many food servers still introduce themselves and recite the daily specials, and restaurants that impose this procedure usually have too many specials to remember. In British Columbia, servers are much less likely to force their affections on customers and the daily specials will usually be photocopied and inserted into the menu, as they should be.

Of basic Canadian courtesy, my friend and fellow travel writer Carol Baker says, "If you step on someone's foot and he or she apologizes, you can be sure you've bumped into a genuine Canadian."

Among the similarities in the region that you aren't as likely to encounter elsewhere in either country are the overall good manners in traffic. You'll seldom hear a car horn anywhere in the Evergreen Triangle, in part because it is considered bad form but also because you can be ticketed for it in Canada. With a few exceptions, you can expect courtesy among drivers. If you use your turn signal well in advance of changing lanes, you can be sure someone will motion you ahead of them. One of the supreme tests of this courtesy is at either entrance to Vancouver's Lions Gate Bridge, where two and sometimes three lanes of traffic are funneled into a single lane. The traffic moves slowly but steadily in all lanes because drivers take turns making the merger smoothly. That isn't always the case in Washington.

The following statement may not do justice to the innate courtesy of Canadians, but one basic difference between the two countries seems to be that the United States celebrates the individual and Canada celebrates the community. I've learned that if a Canadian calls an American a cowboy, it isn't meant to be a compliment, and I think it goes back to the way each country was settled. In the United States the West wasn't settled, it was conquered. It was a wilderness free-for-all with no semblance of civilization; law and order came last. In Canada, the North West Mounted Police were sent out to negotiate with native people, to select townsites, to build a framework of civilization. When that was accomplished, then the settlers were invited to come forth.

Canadians are almost obsessed with the United States while Americans pay little attention to Canada. The former Prime Minister Pierre Trudeau once said that having the United States as a next-door neighbor is "like sleeping with an elephant; you feel every twitch." When an American goes to a dinner party in British Columbia the conversation inevitably comes to an American subject. When a Canadian goes to a dinner party in Washington, Canada is hardly ever mentioned except in passing.

Canadians do not hesitate to comment on American politics at length, sometimes with bitterness or sarcasm, and they are generally as well versed in American national politics as Americans, better versed than many. But a glacial chill will descend on the room if an American criticizes Canadian politicians. I once researched this theory during the 1992 American presidential campaign. After listening to my Canadian friends bash candidate Bill Clinton, I said that I didn't think then-Prime Minister Mulroney was getting fair treatment. A silence descended, then I was told that I shouldn't talk about things I had no way of understanding.

This intense interest in American politics probably has something to do with Peter Jennings and other Canadians working in American television news and entertainment. American news is legitimate news in Canada's media. Once I was visiting a family in the wilderness on the Yukon-British Columbia border. When we listened to the Canadian Broadcasting Corporation's news on the battery-powered radio, I tallied the stories and 40 per cent of the program was devoted to American news. Conversely, the American media generally ignores Canada. An exception is KVOS-TV in Bellingham, which carries up to 50 per cent Canadian news. (Without trying for cynicism, I wonder what the ratio would be without the Canadian advertising.)

Americans take Canada's friendship for granted, and although Canadians know America would defend them to the death against an attack from anyone, this lack of everyday, neighborly interest rankles. On the other hand, if the United States decided to take an active interest in Canada, the resentment would be immediate and acid would drip from journalistic pens and politicians' tongues. To quote another former Prime Minister, Lester B. Pearson, on U.S.-Canadian relations: "We worry when you look hard at us, but we are touchy about being overlooked."

Canada plays an increasingly important role in international affairs. Since it has no "natural enemies" (wouldn't it be wonderful if the United States could say that?), when Canadian troops are sent to political hot spots around the world, they are treated with much more courtesy and respect than those from the United States. Canada does not have a history of meddling in other countries' internal affairs. To be blunt about it, the world trusts Canada. The same can't be said about the United States. Oddly, the large number of Canadians working in entertainment in the States (such as Michael J. Fox, a Vancouver-area lad, Margot Kidder, Martin Short, Donald Sutherland) doesn't bother Americans at all, but it does irk Canadians who have to watch American television to see their home-grown talent. However, as television becomes more international, I think that we will see more Canadians on American television and communications in general will become global rather than national in character.

It is a national law in Canada that 30 per cent of music played on Canadian radio stations must by performed by Canadian artists. This doesn't concern Americans for the very reason the law was enacted: Canada is a very small market. Singers such as Anne Murray, Gordon Lightfoot and Loreena McKennitt obviously love the law.

This rivalry is something like sibling rivalry: One child became rich, powerful, envied and is not always sensitive to its siblings, while the other remained more gentle and polite, sometimes ignored by the family but liked by all. In spite of this, the family ties enable them to ride out the irritating habits of the other.

....

A FRIENDLY WARNING...

Several years ago a friend who used to be a cabin attendant for an airline told me she had a simple way of separating travelers from tourists. Tourists, she said, are obsessed with hotels. Travelers talk about people they have met, incidents, small towns and the culture they encountered.

"The moment someone asks me where I stayed, I lose interest," she said.

That may be a bit extreme, but I must admit that I harbor some of the same impatience. So be aware that the person who wrote this book does not pretend to be a food critic, nor do hotels make me lyrical simply because they are expensive; sometimes I simply want a safe, clean and quiet place to sleep. I am not comfortable with a star or diamond rating system unless it is done by people who have experience in the restaurant or hotel industry, such as the AAA or CAA in North America and the Michelin critics in Europe. Nearly every other critic I read is as interested in telling readers how smart they are as they are discussing the matter at hand. They get in the way.

With this said, I believe that Jurgen Gothe in Vancouver is the best food writer in the entire region. Without having to slog through purple prose and all manner of clever asides, Gothe can be trusted to find out if the restaurant is worth visiting. His food column appears in the *Vancouver Sun*'s Saturday section called the Saturday Review, and he writes wine columns for *Western Living* magazine and *Vancouver Magazine*.

Since I am not a food writer, I try to include places that have established a reputation that stretches back a few years. I don't pretend my listing is complete; it is only a place to start. Otherwise, check the local newspapers and their weekend entertainment sections or ask the concierge, other travelers and shopkeepers.

For lodging I recommend that you join the American or Canadian Automobile Association so you can get their tour books to Washington and Western Canada. Both Washington and British Columbia publish free annual magazine-format booklets listing most of the places to stay. These are available at most information centers on the major highways, at the border crossings and by writing to the addresses given on pages 195-96.

I have tried to gather essential information on each of the three major cities for a good selection of things to see and do, and have suggested routes between the cities so that you won't feel you have to be faithful to freeways. You will find more complete and up-to-date information in local newspapers and in specialized guidebooks listed in the Bibliography. Also, I have not listed exact prices because they change so often, so you should call ahead for them. Most museums and attractions are still reasonably priced, but inflation is with us forever.

THE METRIC MESS

Canada operates on the metric system, as does most of the civilized world. The United States has legally been metric since the 19th century, and in 1975 President Gerald Ford signed another law to make the country metric. Oddly, the law had no timetable so Americans still deal in feet, miles, pounds, etc. No change is in sight.

So be aware that when you see a speed-limit sign in Canada saying the maximum speed is 100, it refers to kilometers not miles per hour, and it translates to 62 miles an hour. Multiply the posted speed limit by 0.6 and you'll be reasonably close.

Here are some common conversions:

To convert	to	multiply by
inches	centimeters	2.54
feet	centimeters	30.48
yards	meters	0.91
miles	kilometers	1.61
quarts	liters	0.95
gallons	liters	3.79
ounces	grams	28.35
pounds	kilograms	0.45

To convert	to	multiply by
millimeters	inches	.04
centimeters	inches	.39
meters	feet	3.28
meters	yards	1.09
kilometers	miles	0.62

NOW, ABOUT ALL THAT RAIN...

Yes, it rains in the Evergreen Triangle; that's why it is ever-green. No, it doesn't rain all the time, or even most of the time. But, yes, it does rain frequently, and the skies are often overcast.

The mild marine climate of the area covered in this book is influenced primarily by the latitude, the distance from the moderating effect of the Pacific Ocean and by the mountainous topography. A rich diversity exists in the small area and results in huge variations in average hours of sunshine, rainfall, snow and average temperatures, sometimes over short distances. For example, the average annual rainfall in White Rock, a small community south of Vancouver near the international border, is 43 inches (1092 mm). Less than 30 miles (50 km) away in North Vancouver, the North Shore mountains force clouds to rise and release their moisture, producing annual rainfall averaging 73 inches (1859 mm).

A similar example occurs in the town of Sequim near Port Angeles on Washington's Olympic Peninsula. Sequim is in the so-called rain shadow, or Blue Hole, of the Olympic Mountains, and while its rainfall is a modest 17 inches (432 mm) a year, less than 50 miles (81 km) away in the heart of the Olympic Range the rainfall is more than 200 inches (5080 mm) a year.

The mixture of marine weather, the dry weather from the interior desert, the mountain ranges, the Arctic effect and several other factors are responsible for a bewildering number of microclimates. For example, I live in Edmonds, about halfway between Seattle and Everett, and the weather is quite different from that in either of the two cities. Weather fronts often collide here, causing more showers—and better scenery on the sound—than in either of the larger towns.

To give you a very generalized description of the climate in the Evergreen Triangle:

Summertime is reliably sunny and warm with a frequent cooling breeze. Temperatures in summer reach average highs in the 70s Fahrenheit (mid-20s Celsius) but evenings can be cool, so sweaters are recommended.

In winter, the region is temperate with temperatures seldom below freezing but with characteristically rainy weather. The amount of rain varies greatly with location relative to local mountain ranges. Parts of the coast receive as much rain as the jungles of South America and they also have the lush, dense forest to match. It is worth remembering that this region has one of only three temperate rain forests in the world; the others are in southern Chile and in New Zealand. Vancouver and Seattle receive more rain than the eastern coast of Vancouver Island, including Victoria, and the Gulf and San Juan Islands.

Winter or summer, the weather is extremely changeable, but not violently so. It is for this reason that few local people check the weather forecast before planning outings. This is also a reason that many locals seldom wear raincoats; heavy mists and drizzles are more common than downpours.

However, this casual attitude toward protection from the rain doesn't extend to the wilderness. Lovers of the outdoors should never be without rain gear and warm protection, even in summer. Every summer inadequately clothed people die of hypothermia in the mountains.

Snow falls most winters at sea level on Vancouver, Seattle and some Vancouver Island regions and lasts from a few hours to a few weeks. The amount and duration of snow increases with the distance from the water, both horizontally and vertically above sea level. Ski resorts north of Vancouver and on Vancouver Island boast—and it is true—that you can ski, golf and take a swim in the ocean all on an early spring day. But you won't see many people taking that swim because the sea is so chilly the year around.

It takes a particular kind of person to enjoy this cool and cloudy climate. Some people find the short, dark winter days depressing while others revel in the mild climate.

GETTING AROUND

By Highway

The distance between Vancouver and Seattle is approximately 138 miles (220 km). The international border, on Interstate 5 and Highway 99, is 31 miles (50 km) from Vancouver. Allow three hours' driving time from downtown Seattle to downtown Vancouver, although the actual driving time depends on how busy the border crossing happens to be. The busiest times are normal rush-hour periods—early morning and early evening, and Fridays and Sundays.

The major motorcoach line is Gray Line of Seattle, which serves all three cities in a series of guided tours, some of which include overnight stays in all three cities in the triangle. Phone 604-384-0233 in Victoria, 206-626-6090 in Seattle and 604-879-3363 in Vancouver. Greyhound Lines also operates busses between Seattle and Vancouver: 604-682-3222 in Vancouver; 206-628-5508 in Seattle. The Seattle/Vancouver Shuttle Bus Service, operated by Quick Coach Lines of Richmond, B.C., runs between Vancouver, the Bellingham airport, the downtown Travelodge in Seattle and Seattle-Tacoma International Airport. Phone 604-244-3744, or Seattle 1-800-665-2122.

By Air

Airlines serving the Evergreen Triangle include: Canadian Airlines, 604-279-6611 or 1-800-426-7000 (Vancouver), 1-800-665-1177 (Seattle), 604-382-6111 (Victoria); Horizon Air 1-800-547-9308 (all three cities); Air B.C. 604-688-5515 or 1-800-663-3721 (Vancouver), 206-730-7171 or 1-800-776-3000 (Seattle), 604-360-9074 (Victoria); Delta 604-682-5933 (Vancouver) or 1-800-221-1212 (all three cities); and United 1-800-241-6522 (all three cities).

By Water

After three years with no auto-ferry service between Seattle and Victoria, good news for the tourist industry came in 1994 when B.C. Ferries began a car-passenger ferry service between Seattle and Victoria. The 190-car, 900-passenger *Royal Victorian* makes the run from mid-

May through mid-September. The ferry leaves Seattle's Pier 48 at 1 P.M. each day, then departs from Victoria's Ogden Point to Seattle at 7:30 A.M. The ferry features a duty-free shop, a dining room, a bar and a children's play area.

Victoria is about 1-1/2 hours by B.C. Ferry from Tsawwassen to Swartz Bay (604-386-3431), 2-1/2 hours from Seattle via Victoria Clipper (206-448-5000).

Nanaimo, 69 miles (111 km) north of Victoria, is two hours from Tsawwassen by B.C. Ferry and 1-1/2 hours from Horseshoe Bay.

The vehicle-carrying ferries are publicly owned, with one major exception: Black Ball Transport runs a ferry service on the steamship *Coho* between Victoria and Port Angeles, making four trips daily during the summer and one trip during the winter. The *Coho* is 361 feet (110 m) long, carries a maximum of 1,000 passengers and up to 130 vehicles.

For information on all Washington ferry routes, call 206-464-6400 in Washington or 604-381-1551 for British Columbia routes. For British Columbia ferry information, call 604-386-3431 on both sides of the border. For information on Black Ball Transport, call 604-386-2202 in B.C. or 206-457-4491 in Washington.

By Rail

Great news for rail fans came in 1993 when Amtrak announced it would again offer passenger service between Seattle and Vancouver by 1995. Other rail service is offered by Canada's VIA Rail, which makes the 140-mile (225-km) daily run from Victoria to Courtenay, north of Nanaimo (and thus not in the Evergreen Triangle). The route is named the Malahat Dayliner and the train leaves Victoria at 8:15 A.M., arrives in Courtenay at about 1 P.M., departs for Victoria again at 1:15 P.M. and arrives at 5:45 P.M.

CROSSING THE BORDER

Going back and forth across the Canadian-United States border is usually a simple matter of waiting for the lines to move, answering a few basic questions and continuing on your way. If you are an American or Canadian citizen, you do not need a passport, only basic identity such as a driver's license. In more than 30 years I've never been asked to produce identification.

You are likely to hear some of these questions when entering either country as a guest:

"Where were you born?"

"Where is your home?"

"How long do you intend to stay?"

"Are you taking any gifts to friends?"

"Are you carrying any firearms or Mace?" (entering Canada).

When you return to your country, you will be asked some basic questions, and occasionally more detailed ones:

"Where do you live?"

"How long were you gone?"

"What did you buy?"

Usually these dialogues take no more than 30 seconds, but sometimes the questioning is more detailed and the lines at the highway crossings may back up for half a mile or more.

Although the agencies are close-mouthed about what makes them pull some people in for further questioning, it is known that they have general profiles and if you do not fit them, you may be detained for questioning. I have seen agents descend on cars, remove the passengers and drive the car into the holding area themselves for a thorough search.

One of the funniest such incidents occurred when a rough-looking man driving an enormous Mercedes Benz entered the U.S. from Canada and was detained for questioning. When he walked into the Customs and Immigration office, a clerk looked up and exclaimed, "Clint Eastwood, what are you doing in here?" The agent who failed to recognize him will live with the story for the rest of his life.

One of my own favorite border incidents occurred when I was returning to the U.S. late at night and the agent fell asleep while questioning me. I cleared my throat loudly, he awoke, looked around and began the questioning all over again. On another crossing a new officer was being trained in the Canadian booth and he wanted to know where I was going in Vancouver, with whom I was going to have dinner, and how we happened to be friends. The woman training him at last whispered something in his ear and he said I could go but that I seemed to have "interesting" friends.

You have nothing to worry about while crossing the border if you don't try to sneak anything across and if you tell the truth. The agents aren't there to make either new friends or new enemies. Answer the questions simply and directly and you'll soon be on your way. If you buy anything on the other side of the border, be sure and keep the sales receipt.

American visitors entering Canada may bring with them duty free for their own consumption 40 ounces (1.1 L) of wine or liquor, or two dozen 12-ounce (355 mL) cans or bottles of beer; a carton of cigarettes, 50 cigars and 2.2 lbs. (1 kg) of manufactured tobacco. Gifts valued at more than $40 are subject to duty. Canadians entering the U.S. have similar privileges.

Americans returning to the U.S. after being in Canada for at least 48 hours may bring back goods valued at $400 duty free, including 40 ounces (1.1 L) of alcoholic beverages and a carton of cigarettes.

Canadians returning home from the U.S. after a 48-hour absence may bring in duty-free goods valued at $100 Canadian, including 40 ounces (1.1 L) of wine or liquor or two dozen cans or bottles of beer, a carton of cigarettes, 50 cigars or 14 ounces (400 g) of manufactured tobacco. Gifts valued at more than $40 Canadian are subject to duty.

The PACE Lane

When you drive across the border you'll undoubtedly note that some cars are whipping past you in the far right lane. Not only that, most don't even stop at the border gate. Don't get irate. It is the result of an effort to speed the steadily slowing border-crossing process, especially for those who travel back and forth several times a week without transporting goods. It is a program called PACE, an acronym for the Pacific Corridor Enterprise Council. By being approved and paying a fee—$25 for U.S. citizens,

$10 for Canadians—you place a sticker on your car windshield and drive through the border in a lane set aside for participants, usually without having to stop.

The system is needed. The five border stations in the Evergreen Triangle have more than 27,000,000 crossings a year. By 1993, more than 50,000 people were enrolled in PACE, and plans are under way to introduce it at the Vancouver International Airport to alleviate the long lines commuters often face when their arrival coincides with flights from Asia and Europe.

Border Lineup Information

While in Canada you may call these numbers to check on the length of lines at the various crossings. All are within prefix 604: Point Roberts, 943-2722; Douglas Crossing (Blaine), 535-9754; Pacific Highway Crossing (commercial crossing east of Blaine), 538-3600; Aldergrove Crossing, 856-2791; Huntington Crossing (Sumas), 856-7704.

While in the U.S. you may call any of these numbers, all area code 206: Blaine Peace Arch, 332-6318; Pacific Highway (Blaine commercial crossing), 332-5771; Point Roberts, 945-2314; Sumas (Huntingdon), 988-2971; Lynden (Aldergrove), 354-2183.

This information is also available on Bellingham radio station KGMI, 790 AM, which broadcasts reports at 5:10 and 6:10 on Friday evenings; on Saturday and Sunday they broadcast border reports every hour on the half-hour, and at other times if a problem develops.

THE GST REBATE

Canada has imposed a seven per cent Goods and Services Tax (GST) on nearly everything sold in the country. However, the Visitor Rebate Program allows foreign visitors to get a refund on the tax for goods you take home and on hotel bills, provided you have been in each lodging establishment less than a month.

The rebate does not apply on taxes paid on services, goods left in Canada, restaurant meals, campground fees, automotive fuel, alcohol and tobacco, used goods that tend to increase in value such as artwork and coins, or goods without GST, such as groceries and prescription drugs.

To get the rebate, you must produce the original receipt (not a photocopy) with your form, which you claim at a participating duty-free shop at the border or mail to Ottawa.

TELEPHONES

You'll have no trouble using the telephones in either country because the telephones themselves and the telephone systems are identical. Phoning across the border is simply a matter of placing a long-distance call. The only difference is that pay phones in the U.S. usually will not accept Canadian coins while U.S. coins work in Canadian telephones.

The area code for all of British Columbia is 604.

The area code for most Washington numbers is 206. After January 1995, the 206 area code will be in effect for the area between Tacoma (Fort Lewis, to be exact), Seattle and Everett. The remainder of Washington north of Everett and west of the Cascades will be area code 360.

Outdoor cafés, like this one in >
Seattle's historic Pioneer Square,
are a common sight throughout
the Evergreen Triangle
SEATTLE-KING COUNTY NEWS BUREAU

Seattle

CAFE FE

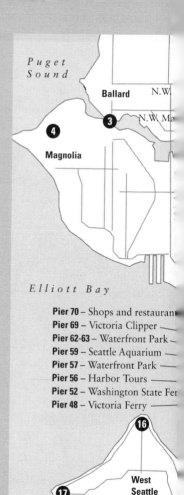

Puget Sound

Ballard

N.W.

3

N.W. Ma

4

Magnolia

Elliott Bay

Pier 70 – Shops and restaurant

Pier 69 – Victoria Clipper ——

Pier 62-63 – Waterfront Park —

Pier 59 – Seattle Aquarium ——

Pier 57 – Waterfront Park ——

Pier 56 – Harbor Tours ——

Pier 52 – Washington State Fer

Pier 48 – Victoria Ferry ——

16

17

West Seattle

California Ave. S.W.

N

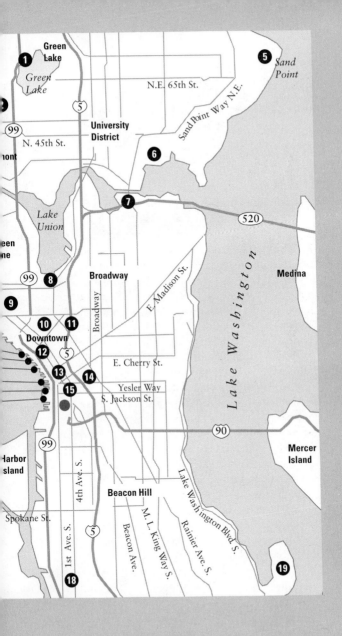

Although it sounds like something a former Miss America might say, the average Seattleite genuinely wants to lead a normal, boring life again. Most old-timers came to Seattle because it was such an anonymous place and was as far as you could go away from home without a passport. Before its discovery by the rest of North America, the average Seattle resident was reserved, perhaps a bit shy, liked the frequent rain and believed that the perfect summer day was overcast and no more than 70 degrees Fahrenheit.

In spite of this Greta Garbo-ish "I vant to be a lawn" posture, Seattle does have several things to be proud of. Some of the world's best commercial airplanes (Boeing) are built here. Some of its merchandising companies (Nordstrom's and Eddie Bauer) and airlines (Alaska and Horizon) became famous for their service. Seattle more or less invented the coffee craze (has anyone not yet heard of Starbucks?) that has swept the west coast of North America and is spreading east like a benign mental condition. Nobody is quite sure how it happened, but Seattle has gone over the edge with coffee. All over town you will find carts serving espresso, latté and other popular caffeine products; outside department stores, at busy street intersections, in lobbies of large buildings. There are even drive-through coffee stands. Seattle is so crazy about caffeine that it has been named Lattéland by the city's best columnist, Jean Godden of the *Seattle Times*. This actually is the third in a series of beverage-related crazes here. The first was the emergence of Washington wineries, and the state has around 50 now doing very well. Then came micro-brewery rage, and now we have micro coffee roasters sprouting up. What next? ask the trend watchers with a sigh.

Then there's the music. The city's new form of music called Grunge has made a big impact among teenagers across the country and made almost instant millionaires of several rock bands. It has a harder edge to the lyrics than one would expect from a city with a reputation for being subdued, but teenagers everywhere are sometimes attracted to self-pity and see life as a negative experience. This attitude was never more apparent than when Kurt Cobain, singer for the band Nirvana, committed suicide in April, 1994.

Like Vancouver, Seattle by itself isn't a large city. Its population is only 516,000 compared with Vancouver's 477,800 and Victoria's 71,000, but Seattle is surrounded by smaller towns whose boundaries have blurred while the population of the whole area has grown to about 2 million. Its best known neighbors are Mercer Island, Bellevue and Kirkland, all three of which are either in the middle of Lake Washington (Mercer Island) or on its eastern side. The northern reaches of the Seattle area have continued spreading until it is connected to Everett 15 miles (24 km) to the north, and south almost to Tacoma, 30 miles (48 km) away.

After all the attention Seattle has received, and the new buildings that have given Seattle a memorable skyline, only the **Pike Place Markets** have remained much as they always were. They will probably stay that way because Seattleites continue to guard them with the fervor of a doting parent protecting a child. The cluster of buildings clings to the edge of a cliff like barnacles to a stone with scores of stalls for food, artwork and trinkets, and is Seattle's most cherished attraction.

The markets have been going almost since the turn of the century. They were recently the center of a lawsuit when a limited partnership bought several of the buildings (the partners were from New York, which is only slightly worse to local paranoiacs than California), but the locals went to court and won. Thus the markets will remain the same: funky, cluttered, noisy and out of character for the rest of rather straitlaced, tidy-minded Seattle.

The new $60 million-plus **Seattle Art Museum** was built only a block from the markets. It is getting a mixed reaction from locals, but most of the reviews from across North America have been raves for both the architecture and the exhibits that have been taken out of storage and at last presented.

The other downtown attraction that Seattle wants to keep unchanged is **Pioneer Square**. This area, once the heart of the city, deteriorated into a seedy area, then a

The Space Needle, built ∧
during the 1962 World's Fair,
is Seattle's visual symbol.
SEATTLE-KING COUNTY NEWS BUREAU

trendy restoration project revived the neighborhood. Now it is back to its original use as a combination work place and nightlife center. In addition to the many shops, restaurants and art galleries, Elliott Bay Books is one of the finest bookstores on the West Coast.

The **International District** is only three or four blocks east of Pioneer Square. Although not nearly as elaborate as that in Vancouver, the district has a large number of Chinese, Korean, Vietnamese and Japanese restaurants, and various Asian and Pacific Rim shops.

The **Kingdome** is only a block south of Pioneer Square. Here the National Football League Seahawks and the American League Mariners play. If you want to hang out with the sports crowd, the cavernous F.X. McRory's Steak, Chop and Oyster House in Pioneer Square is the place to go after Kingdome games, or to watch pay-cable prize fights.

A word of advice: Pioneer Square is America's original Skid Road. Don't even think of calling it Skid Row in Seattle; that's worse than calling the City By The Bay Frisco. The name came during the pioneer years when logs were skidded down the hillside to Henry Yesler's sawmill on the waterfront and the street was called Skid Road. That bit of hobo history is kept alive by the numbers of street people you will encounter; Seattle has a long tradition of tolerance toward the down-and-out.

Farther down the hill you will arrive at **the waterfront,** which is gradually becoming a place for tourists rather than working ships and boats. The numbers of shops, parks and restaurants are increasing, and it is rapidly losing its tangy smells of creosote and fish. The main section runs about half a mile from Pier 56, where the cross-sound ferries dock, to Pier 70, now a collection of shops and restaurants. Pier 70 is the southern end of a long strip of a park named Myrtle Edwards, popular with noon-hour joggers and picnickers, which runs along the beach to Pier 90.

In the half-mile of the downtown waterfront you will find the boats for harbor tours, the Seattle Aquarium, an Omnidome theater, the fast boats to Victoria, B.C., several fine restaurants and the Waterfront Park, where you can sit and fish and watch the world go by. In fact, the only hotel on the waterfront, the Edgewater Inn, will lend you fishing tackle if you want to fish from your window.

You don't have to walk the whole length of the waterfront. The city bought three retired electric tramways from Melbourne, Australia, refurbished them and put them on railroad tracks running along the waterfront from the International District to Pier 70.

Seattle Center is the third major downtown attraction. This is where the world's fair was held in 1962 and the site now is the cultural and recreational center of the city. Here you will find the Opera House, two stage theaters, the Coliseum where the NBA SuperSonics play, a carnival-ride area, several exhibition halls, outdoor stages for summer festivals, the Pacific Science Center, and the Center House with its collection of ethnic and fast-food restaurants and various shops.

Two of Seattle's most successful festivals are held in the center. Memorial Day weekend features the Northwest Folklife Festival, the largest folk festival in America. It has lots of folk and ethnic music, dance, crafts, poetry readings and food. The other major festival is Bumbershoot on Labor Day weekend which celebrates the arts, live and graphic.

The Seattle Center is also the home of the **Space Needle,** Seattle's most photographed feature. The Needle now has two restaurants, the original at the top of the 520-foot (1705-m) tower and a new one at a much lower elevation. Next to taking a ride in a float plane from Lake Union, a visit to the top of the Space Needle is the best way to orient yourself to Seattle.

Seattle has a long-standing reputation for excellent live theater and supports a surprisingly large number of theater groups: the professional Seattle Repertory Theater, Intiman, A Contemporary Theater, The Empty Space, several specialty companies (Gilbert & Sullivan Society and childrens' theater groups, for example) and a number of small experimental groups.

You may not come to Seattle just to take in a movie, but Seattle has one of the widest selections of movie houses on the West Coast. It has a reputation for being one of the most sophisticated film cities in the country, and Hollywood often tries out films in Seattle before making the final edit and sending them out into the world. Thus, it rankles Seattle film buffs to see a film about Seattle—made in Vancouver. They're shot there for the very good reason that Vancouver works harder at making the city attractive to studios in terms of production costs and local facilities.

In addition to the standard Hollywood fare, smaller theaters specialize in revivals of classics, foreign films and lesser-known films. The Seattle International Film Festival in May and the Vancouver International Film Festival in October help introduce new films and dig out some oldies that deserve a showing.

Still, it is natural beauty more than anything else that attracts most people to Seattle, and Puget Sound is one of the most beautiful stretches of inland saltwater in North America. Puget Sound is almost everyone's favorite, as the prices of waterfront or view property prove. Instead of the empty ocean seen along most of the West Coast, on Puget Sound sailboats, windsurfers, rowboats, tugs, barges, ferryboats, charter boats, fishing boats, military ships, cargo ships, and many other kinds of vessels form a constantly changing backdrop to the city.

The Washington State Ferries are an extension of the state's highway system. They stretch from the Seattle area to the islands and the mainland on the west side of the sound. A pleasant way to spend a couple of hours is to buy picnic makings at the Pike Place Market, or any deli, and board the ferry to Bremerton, a two-hour round trip. Other ferries from Seattle go to Bainbridge Island and Vashon Island, both of which are havens for the independent-minded who like living within sight of Seattle, knowing that the inconvenience of ferry commuting keeps island population under control.

Seattle is only an hour's drive from the four ski areas on Snoqualmie Pass, reached by Interstate 90. During the summer the area is popular with both day hikers and backpackers. Mount Rainier National Park is only 60 miles (96 km) away. The park has good roads along its southern and eastern sides, good lodging both inside and outside the park, and several first-rate campgrounds.

The other two national parks, Olympic and North Cascades, are not so easily toured in a short time from Seattle and you should plan on several days for each. However, you don't have to leave the city limits for forests because Seattle's park system preserves several enclaves of wilderness inside the city limits. The **Washington Park Arboretum** is a combination of waterways and marshes, popular with people renting canoes from the University of Washington. The arboretum also has many acres of trees and plants, including a formal Japanese Garden.

The most popular city park is **Green Lake**, a small lake with a 2.8-mile (4.5 km) pathway around it that is always busy with walkers, joggers, roller skaters, bicyclists and sitters there to watch the parade. Green Lake adjoins the **Woodland Park Zoo** which is frequently praised for its African savanna where animals have more space and privacy than usual.

One reason *Bicycling* magazine rated Seattle as the best city in the country for biking is the **Burke Gilman Trail,** a refurbished railroad track that runs 12.5 miles (20 km) from Lake Union through the University of Washington campus north along the shore of Lake Washington to its very tip. From there you must face the traffic on a busy two-lane highway to Bothell and catch the Samammish River Trail, which goes through a peaceful countryside, with a bonus stop possible at the Chateau Ste. Michelle and Columbia Crest wineries.

Getting around Seattle is easy because its core is confined to the area between Lake Washington and Puget Sound. The public transportation system, Metro, has a new tunnel beneath Third Avenue, and you can ride free in the downtown core between Battery Street on the north, Jackson Street on the south, and Sixth Avenue on the east, either through the tunnel or on other surface busses. Unfortunately, you must pay 75 cents to ride the trolley that runs from the International District through Pioneer Square and along the Waterfront to Pier 70.

Streets north of downtown are so designated—N. 45th, for example, and the same applies to those south of downtown. Highway 99 (also named Aurora Avenue) is the dividing line between streets designated Northeast and Northwest. First Avenue South performs that duty south of the city, except that the streets are either Southwest or South; there's no Southeast designation.

Driving in Seattle isn't fun. The city's hour-glass shape bisected north-and-south by Interstate 5 with spurs leading off on the two floating bridges across Lake Washington has made the city very congested. In fact, a recent study showed that Seattle's traffic was the fifth worst in the United States.

SIGHTSEEING and GUIDED TOURS

Hiram M. Chittenden Locks (Ballard Locks)

The most popular tourist attraction in Seattle isn't the Space Needle or Pioneer Square or even the Pike Place Markets. It is the Hiram M. Chittenden Locks, better known as the Ballard Locks, located in a neighborhood that has a distinctly Scandinavian flavor. One reason for the locks' popularity might be that it is a free show; even parking along N.W. 54th is free.

All boats going between Puget Sound and Lakes Union

Seattle's most popular tourist ∧
attraction: the Hiram M.
Chittenden Locks in Ballard.
PHOTO BY ARCHIE SATTERFIELD

and Washington must pass through the locks. This mixture of pleasure and commercial boats brings all kinds of vessels to the locks—trawlers and gill-netters on their way to Alaska, tugs towing log booms to sawmills, ships enroute to berths on the lakes—and makes the locks the equivalent of a daily maritime parade. You can watch it from close-up at the locks themselves, or from the grassy lawn on the hillside overlooking them. You'll probably marvel at the patience of the lock employees who shepherd novices through with the old pros.

Nearly 2 million visitors stroll through the seven-acre **Carl S. English Jr. Botanical Garden** each year. The garden is part of the locks and is named for the employee who began the garden as a hobby. It has species from all over the world mingled with the native Pacific Northwest plants. A self-guided tour goes through the gardens; a one-hour guided tour includes both the garden and the locks. Information: 206-783-7059.

Pike Place Markets

Several years ago the great Northwest painter Mark Tobey said that the Pike Place Markets were the soul of Seattle. If that is no longer true—Seattle has changed a great deal lately and you'll find almost as many gift shops as food stalls—these public markets are still a "must" for visitors. They are still real enough for many residents to make at least one visit there a week for produce and fish and the pleasure of being in an untraditional place in a quite traditional city.

The markets are on a two-plus-block-long street that curves northward at the western end of Pike Street. Originally they were built on stilts and dangled out over the edge of a bluff that looks across Elliott Bay. They have been stabilized in recent years, but the ramshackle feeling remains. A number of the market's restaurants offer excellent views from windows facing west, and elevators have been added to make it easier to move between the markets and the waterfront.

The public markets started in 1907 as a place where vegetable and fruit growers gathered to sell their produce to city dwellers. As industries took over their farm lands for factories and parking lots, the farmers were replaced by gift stores, jewelry stores, restaurants, antique shops and a variety of specialty shops. Today, more than one hundred shops, individuals, produce sellers, and even a modern bank operate at the west end of Pike Street and in the main arcade facing Pike Place from both sides.

Among the most popular attractions are the fish-market employees who entertain visitors by throwing generously sized fish back and forth while keeping up an amusing patter. And the most popular place to meet a friend for lunch is "at the pig," an enormous bronze pig at the foot of Pike Place.

Maritime Heritage Center

1000 Valley St. This park on the south end of Lake Union between Fairview Avenue and Westlake Avenue is being expanded to tell part of the Puget Sound maritime history. Two major organizations operate beneath its umbrella:

The **Center for Wooden Boats,** 1010 Valley St. (206-382-2628), exhibits several original wooden vessels and replicas of others, including dugout canoes and various kayaks and sailboats. Canoes, kayaks and sailboats may be rented there. Free.

Northwest Seaport, 1002 Valley St. (206-447-9800), is home port for the *Wawona,* the remains of an 1897 sailing schooner. Admission.

Seattle Center

(Information, call 206-684-8582.) This vast public area on the edge of downtown Seattle, between Denny Way and Mercer Street, is a gift from the 1962 World's Fair. Before the fair, it was a mixed neighborhood of rundown businesses and modest homes with a playfield and armory in the middle. Now it is one of Seattle's busiest places and one of the nicest things that have happened to the city. Here are its major components:

The **Pacific Science Center.** Its shallow pools with famous arches as a signature make the Science Center second only to the Space Needle in visual impact; many people like the Science Center better. The Center has been very successful in its mission of making science fun for all ages. It has the Eames/IMAX Theater where films are shown and conferences held; the Sea Monster House, a replica of a Northwest Indian ceremonial house; an area where visitors can operate computers and play games; full-scale models of manned and unmanned spacecraft; the Star Lab shows, an 8,000 square foot (743 square metre) overhead domed screen that shows the galaxies.

The Balcony Book and Gift Shop stocks nature and science books, puzzles, toys and Native American crafts.

Center House. This is probably the most heavily used building in the Center. Visitors from years past will remember it as the Food Circus Building. It is filled with shops, meeting rooms, fast-food outlets, and the Center administrative offices.

Coliseum. The home of the Seattle SuperSonics is also used for rock concerts and trade shows.

Opera House. At least for the moment, this is the home of the Seattle Symphony and the Seattle Opera. A new symphony hall will soon be built on the opposite side of Mercer Street.

Playhouse. This is the original home of the Seattle Repertory Theater and is now used by the Intiman Theater and the Gilbert & Sullivan Society. It seats 890 and has a beautifully landscaped courtyard. Frequent exhibits of photography and art are hung in the lobby.

Bagley Wright Theater. This $10 million theater, paid for in part with private donations, is one of the nation's largest resident professional theaters, and is the new home of the Seattle Repertory Theater. It seats 864.

Arena. This plain-jane hall is used for conventions, high-school graduation exercises and other large meetings.

Mural Amphitheater. Hundreds of musical groups and dance troupes have performed on this large outdoor stage area with its giant mosaic mural, "The Seattle Scene" by Paul Horiuchi. The stage is surrounded by a pool and grass amphitheater. Free concerts are held here.

International Fountain. Electronically operated and lighted, the fountain plays a constantly changing pattern of water accompanied by music.

Flag Plaza Pavilion. The pavilion was a popular spot during the Seattle World's Fair and now is used for exhibits, flower shows, festivals and similar special events.

Alweg Monorail. When the monorail was built during the World's Fair held here in 1962, many residents assumed it would eventually be extended from downtown Seattle to Seattle-Tacoma International Airport. But the monorail didn't make a big hit with businesses along Fifth Avenue in its shadow, and the extension never happened and probably never will. Today it runs back and forth along a 1.2-mile (2-km) track from the Seattle Center to Westlake Mall, between 4th and 5th and Pine. It makes the trip in 90 seconds, and offers shoppers and visitors the alternative of parking near the center and riding the monorail to and from downtown, even if the ride isn't memorable.

Seattle Aquarium

Seattle's Aquarium north of Waterfront Park on Pier 59 (206-386-4320) offers an up-close look at Puget Sound marine life with displays re-creating shore and underwater habitats. It was the first aquarium in the world built to be connected directly to life in the ocean. You literally go into an underwater world shared with Puget Sound sea life—sharks, several species of salmon, perch, rockfish, flounder, cod, octopuses, sculpins, starfish, barnacles, and shellfish. It also houses ducks, wrens, sea stars, and crabs in a salt marsh, beach and pond. A tide rises and falls to expose barnacles, mussels, and similar shellfish at tide lines. Open daily. Also found here is the small Museum of Sea and Ships. Admission.

Washington Park Arboretum

Along Lake Washington Boulevard between Highway 520 and Madison Street (206-543-8800 or 325-4510). This is one of the most beautiful places in Seattle, and as beautiful places should be, the Arboretum is designed for people to enjoy it. The 200-acre (81-ha) nature preserve is located in Washington Park on Lake Washington Blvd. near the University of Washington. One of the most popular sections is the Japanese Garden which is heavily visited in the spring and fall. Its teahouse and pond was designed and built by Japanese landscape architects and a tea ceremony is held there the third Sunday of each month. The Japanese Garden is open daily in the summer, on weekends in the winter. Admission. For information on the tea ceremonies, call 206-684-4725.

Virtually all types of Pacific Northwest ornamental plants are displayed throughout the Arboretum along with the city's largest collection of plants from all over the world. The Waterfront Trail connects to the Foster Island Nature Trail near the Museum of History and Industry. Other popular trails are Azalea Way and Loderi Valley. Arboretum volunteers offer a variety of tours, depending on the season, and occasional plant sales. For information on tours and plant sales, call 206-543-8800. Open until sunset the year-round; free.

Alaska Sightseeing Tours

Fourth Avenue and Battery Bldg. (206-441-8687). Due to the federal laws prohibiting foreign-built passenger ships from traveling between American ports without touching on a foreign port between, all of the two dozen or more American cruise ships working the Inside Passage must depart from Vancouver, British Columbia. This company's small ships are the first American-built ships to leave Seattle for Alaska in decades. Most of them call at Victoria, Ketchikan, Petersburg and Sitka. The company's first vessel is the *Spirit of Alaska*, a 158-foot (48-m) vessel with 40 outside cabins, bow thrusters and a ramp to permit landings on wilderness beaches.

Seattle Name Droppers

(206-625-1317) This is an unusual tour for Seattle because its citizens take pride in ignoring the famous or at least leaving them alone. However, the three-hour tour is popular with tourists, and on it you can see where Ray Charles, Jimi Hendrix, Judy Collins and Quincy Jones got their starts; where Bruce Lee, Howard Duff, Carol Channing, Gypsy Rose Lee and Jean Smart lived; where Alice B. Toklas and Frank Herbert hung out and where Tom Robbins still appears; the Wah Mee Massacre site, and where mass-murderer Ted Bundy lived.

Spirit of Puget Sound

Pier 70 (206-443-1442). This three-decker boat takes up to 600 passengers on cruises around Elliott Bay and out into Puget Sound. It is best known for its buffet dinners followed by a floor show and dancing. More popular with groups than individuals, although couples are certainly welcome.

Gray Line of Seattle

(206-624-5813) This largest tour company in Seattle offers a wide selection of escorted bus and boat tours, including two-hour and six-hour narrated tours of Seattle. Specialty tours such as the Chocolate and Wine Sampler make stops at a chocolate factory and a winery. Pickup at several downtown hotels is included. Also offered are overnight trips to Victoria, Mt. Rainier, Mt. St. Helens and the Olympic Peninsula. During the summer months, Gray Line runs a motorized trolley in the downtown district that connects the major hotels with Pioneer Square and the waterfront. It also has a Northwest Triangle Tour that covers almost all of the area described in this book.

Victoria Clipper

Pier 69 (206-448-5000). Although talk continues about large ships running between Seattle and Victoria, only the Victoria Clipper offers water-borne passenger-only transportation between Seattle and Victoria. The company runs water-jet-powered catamarans on the route daily: three round-trips during the summer, one trip during the winter months, and two trips during the spring and fall seasons. The catamarans are fast—15 to 31 knots—so the trip takes only two and a half hours. They also make special trips around Puget Sound, to La Conner during the height of the tulip season, and scheduled dinner cruises.

Bill Speidel's Underground Tour

Doc Maynard's Public House, First and James (206-682-4646). This is one of Seattle's oldest and most eccentric tours. It shows the part of Pioneer Square, once the ground floor of businesses, that became basements when the level of streets was raised. The guides dispense a lot of Seattle lore that stretches the truth in a harmless manner.

Blake Island and Tillicum Village

Pier 56 (206-329-5700). This is probably Seattle's most popular tour because it combines a beautiful boat ride, a tour of the waterfront, an excellent salmon dinner, and authentic Native American dances. The 473-acre (191-ha) Blake Island lies between Vashon and Bainbridge islands and is owned entirely by the State Parks Department for use as a marine park. Tillicum Village is a concession on the island. The longhouse-style building will seat 1,000. In addition to the delicious salmon, baked over an alder wood fire until it is brown after being basted in lemon butter, the menu consists of tossed salad, relishes, baked potato in foil, green beans almondine, hot bread, wild blackberry tart, and soft drinks. During the meal, Native American dancers perform traditional interpretative dances on a large stage decorated with totemic art. A craft shop is in the lobby, and carvers frequently work on totems and smaller items in the longhouse.

Argosy Tours

Pier 56 (206-623-1445). Three boats—the *Barbary Coast*, the *Harbor Tourist* and the *Goodtime*—make one-hour tours along Seattle's waterfront, the Ballard Locks, Lake Union and Lake Washington. Tours begin at Pier 56 and

Tillicum Village prepares salmon in >
the manner of Native Americans.
TILLICUM VILLAGE

cruise north to Pier 90 below Magnolia Bluff, then back south to the Harbor Islands shipyards. Half of the boats' seats are on open decks, so it is wise to bring warm clothing. Season: May 1 to late September. Senior citizens' rates available. Special Japanese language tours are also available.

Parks

Seattle has dozens of fine parks and keeps adding more as public lands become available. While the city has suffered from the demise of the Cold War in terms of losing defense jobs, it has become richer from the addition of Fort Lawton (Discovery Park) and the Sand Point Naval Air Station (Warren G. Magnuson Park). When a gas-manufacturing plant was closed, Seattle turned it into the Gas Works Park, and when a railroad was abandoned, it became the Burke Gilman Trail along Lake Washington. Everyone hated Interstate 5 roaring through the center of the city, so a lid was placed on part of it to build the Freeway Park. Other parks were created early in the city's history, such as Green Lake and Lincoln.

Here are some of the more interesting or unusual parks.

Waterfront Park. Pier 55. This island of peace beneath the Alaskan Way Viaduct and beside the busy waterfront and Elliott Bay docks still manages to have an overall feeling of quietness. It offers great views across Elliott Bay, and Seattleites love it because it is near their jobs—only a short distance from the end of University or Union streets. Here you can watch the water traffic and the Olympics while eating a leisurely lunch. A glass-enclosed public viewing gallery with an outside deck is at the end of Pier 57, and the promenade extends to the Aquarium.

Discovery Park. The main gate is at W. Government Way and 36th Avenue W. This is one of the thousands of military bases around the country that have been turned into public areas. In this case, it was Fort Lawton for decades until it became apparent that Seattle was not going to be invaded from the sea. Its peninsula covers nearly 400 acres (161 ha) of Magnolia Bluff and includes 2 miles (3.2 km) of beaches, isolated forested ravines, small streams, and meadows.

Motorized vehicles are banned from the park except for designated parking areas. A half-mile "paracours" or health path with 15 exercise stations winds through the timber. Daybreak Star, an Indian cultural center where you can watch Indian craftsmen at work, is located just inside the main gate. Along the beach area the Coast Guard operates the West Point Light Station, open in the afternoons for tours. Discovery Park is open daily from dawn to dusk. Headquarters: 3801 W. Government Way. Phone: 206-386-4236.

Green Lake. Across Aurora from Woodland Park Zoo at 60th Street, this is one of Seattle's most popular parks. The paved path around it is so heavily used that traffic jams are becoming a problem as walkers, strollers, joggers, roller skaters and bicycle riders compete for space on the path. During the warmer months you can rent canoes, small sailboats and paddle boats. A large indoor swimming pool and playfields are at the east end of the lake, and areas are set aside on the west end for radio-powered boats.

Woodland Park Zoo. Phinney Avenue N. between N. 50th and N. 59th streets. Consistently ranked as one of the best zoos in America, the Woodland Park Zoo has for the past several years been trying to become a model zoo with an emphasis on preserving endangered species and treating the animals with respect. Among its features are the Nocturnal Houses that reverse night and day and the Swamp and Marsh with ponds and outdoor aviary filled with ducks, herons, coots and other water birds. Gorillas roam through a tropical forest with streams, boulders, natural soils, and ample trees for climbing, and Asian monkeys swing in trees on tropical forest islands and charge across waterfalls to chase other simians. The latest addition is the African savanna which has lions, hippos, pata monkeys, giraffes, zebras, springboks, a walk-through aviary and land and water birds. The zoo opens at 8:30 every morning of the year. Closing time varies from 4:00 to 6:00 in the evening, according to the season. Schools and other groups: call 206-684-4800 for admission fees and tour information.

Gas Works Park. Pacific Avenue at the north end of Lake Union. The park comes by its name honestly: part of its permanent exhibits are the futuristic remains of a plant for manufacturing heating and lighting gas that were an eyesore on Lake Union's skyline for years. The park was controversial when it was built because of the contraptions from the gas plant it preserved. Now, of course, everyone loves the rusting hulks. The mound built beside the park gives an unobstructed view of the city skyline, and is a favorite place for kite flyers to launch their kites. Also, a huge concrete aggregate and bronze sundial was built flat on the ground so that you can stand in the middle and your shadow will mark the hour.

An old boiler house with an overhead maze of pipes has been turned into a play barn, including a picnic shelter that can be reserved for large groups. Many of the discarded pumps, large machinery, and equipment pieces painted in bright colors may seem spooky and grotesque, but children, who understand these things, find it entertaining.

Freeway Park. Dangling out over Interstate 5 in the heart of the city, this park is bordered by Sixth Avenue, Spring Street, Eighth Avenue and University Street. This is one of the best cures for the eight-lane Interstate 5 freeway that roars through the heart of Seattle. With that concrete river canyon splitting the city in half, the park was created to tie the city back together and to provide a place for people to relax, to eat a brown-bag lunch, to sit beneath trees in a completely urban area.

A big lid was built over the freeway to create a 5.4-acre (2.2-ha) platform, then tons of concrete were poured, acres of lawn added along with groundcovers, pathways, plazas, fountains, and waterfalls. To everyone's delight, and surprise, the sound of the waterfalls and fountains plus the screens of trees and shrubs muffle the roar of the freeway traffic.

It was all such a good idea that the city and state next built the Washington State Convention and Trade Center nearby, also over the freeway.

Myrtle Edwards and **Elliott Bay Parks.** From Pier 71 to

Pier 86. These adjoining parks have a 1.25-mile (2-km) pathway along a stretch of waterfront that was once quite ugly. Benches were placed beside the pathway, shade trees planted, and grassy areas created for kite flying. The pathway parallels the waterfront past the massive grain elevators that block the Queen Anne Hill view of Elliott Bay and continues on to Pier 86, the import-car terminal (Lemon Grove, as some wags call it). Myrtle Edwards Park at the southern end adjoins Pier 70. This park has the controversial lumps of stone some consider sculpture and others consider, well, lumps of stone.

THOSE MAGNIFICENT MALLS

Covered shopping malls are one of Seattle's gifts to the United States if not the world—Northgate was the first in the country. Since then they have proliferated like dandelions and have siphoned off shoppers from the downtown area. Most shops in these malls accept Candian currency without hesitation. That isn't always the case everywhere in Washington.

Northgate, Interstate 5 and North 105th Street—with 116 stores and more than 350,000 shoppers each week, making it the most heavily used in the Seattle area. Sales average $200 million a year.

Southcenter, Interstate 5 and southern end of Interstate 405—with 127 stores and 275,000 to 300,000 shoppers each week. Gross sales are about $250 million annually.

Alderwood Mall, Interstate 5 and northern end of Interstate 405—136 stores. (Figures on sales and number of shoppers are unavailable.)

Sea-Tac Mall, Pacific Highway South and South 320th Street—106 stores. About $50 million gross annual sales and 40,000 to 50,000 shoppers each week.

Bellevue Square, Northeast 8th Street and Bellevue Way—198 stores with some 182,000 shoppers each week. $275 million gross annual sales.

SEATTLE HOTELS

In most of Seattle's hotels you will find service for which the city is so well known. It wasn't always this way, of course, and it wasn't too many years ago that not only did few Seatleites know how to pronounce concierge, even fewer knew what one was. Now all the major hotels have them. The competition in the downtown area is intense so customers are the winners while hotels search for new ways to make visits pleasant. Not all hotel guests want a lot of interaction with the staff; sometimes they just want a clean, quiet, safe and reasonably priced place to sleep. So this selection covers some of the best hotels in all price ranges.

Code: Inexpensive – $60 and less; Moderate – $60 to $100; Expensive – $100 and up.

∧ *Sailboat heels to the wind as it skims over Lake Union, against a backdrop of Seattle's downtown office buildings.*
Seattle-King County News Bureau

Downtown

Alexis Hotel, First Avenue and Madison Street (206-624-4844). This hotel, which everyone calls European-style, was designed more for the quiet, the circumspect and the wealthy, most definitely not for convention-goers with funny hats. The 54-room hotel offers whirlpool bathtubs, real fireplaces in some suites and an excellent restaurant. Continental breakfasts. *Expensive*.

Best Western Executive Inn – 200 Taylor St. N. (206-448-9444). This motel is one of the most convenient places to stay if you are going to spend much time in the Seattle Center. It is an easy walk from the Monorail and is on the edge of the free zone for Metro busses. It has 123 units, some with refrigerators, and a garage. *Moderate*.

Best Western Loyal Inn, 2301 Eighth Ave. (206-682-0200). This, too, is near the Seattle Center with 90 units, sauna, whirlpool and near a restaurant. *Inexpensive.*

Crowne Plaza, Sixth Avenue and Seneca Street (206-464-1980). Don't let the plain lobby discourage you because this former Hilton has spacious and airy lounges above the lobby on the 12th floor. Excellent views of the city and sound, and within walking distance to anywhere downtown. *Expensive.*

Econo Lodge, 325 Aurora Ave. N. (206-441-0400). Four of the 58 units have kitchens, and 19 have refrigerators. Close to the downtown area. *Inexpensive.*

Edgewater Inn, Pier 67 (206-728-7000). This is another good buy for the location, virtually hanging out over Puget Sound. It is actually Seattle's only true waterfront hotel. One of the hotel's favorite gimmicks is that they'll supply the fishing tackle if you want to drop a line out of your window. *Expensive.*

Four Seasons Olympic, Fourth Avenue and University Street (206-621-1700). This is Seattle's only hotel to earn a five-star rating from the AAA. After many years as the city's major hotel and the original flagship of Western International Hotels, the forerunner of Westin, the Olympic was getting old and showing it. Then the Canadian company Four Seasons took over the lease, refurbished and made several changes, including opening up its original curved driveway off University, and added a couple of excellent restaurants. Its Garden Court is one of those places you will want to meet friends for a drink at the end of the day and the beginning of a promising evening. *Expensive.*

Inn at the Market, First Avenue and Pine Street (206-443-3600). One of Seattle's most sophisticated hotels, this one overlooks the Pike Place Markets and Elliott Bay. Although it is sometimes billed as a bed-and-breakfast, it is much more of a hotel than the traditional B&B. It has 65 rooms with a central courtyard ringed by shops and the good restaurant, Champagne. A rooftop deck and coffee shop round out the amenities. *Expensive.*

The Inn at Virginia Mason, 1006 Spring St. (206-583-6453). This small hotel began as something of an inexpensive guesthouse for families of patients in the Virginia Mason Hospital, but has recently branched out to attract the general public. Very quiet neighborhood and pleasant rooms. Restaurant. *Moderate.*

Mayflower Park Hotel, 405 Olive Way (206-623-8700). This small hotel is one of the downtown jewels that is sometimes overlooked. Its location couldn't be better for those who love things urban: it is right across the street from the Bon Marché and just down the street from Nordstrom's and the new square and shopping area called Westlake Center. The rooms were recently refurbished and the windows are double-paned to cut the street noise. Garage. *Expensive.*

Residence Inn by Marriott, 800 Fairview Ave. N. (206-624-6000). This new hotel is convenient to the restaurants and shops on the west end of Lake Union and just off the Mercer Street Exit of Interstate 5. Of the 234 units, 54 have two bedrooms and kitchens. Heated pool, saunas, exercise room and garage. *Expensive.*

Hotel Seattle, 315 Seneca St. (206-623-5110). Recently renovated, this smallish (81 rooms) hotel is near the Federal Building, the Main Public Library and the financial district. Restaurant and cocktail lounge. Garage one block away. *Moderate.*

Sheraton Hotel, Sixth Avenue and Pike Street (206-621-9000). Designed primarily for convention business, you may stumble over luggage in the spacious lobby that has a truly great collection of Pilchuck Glass. But this establishment is one of Seattle's best. It made immediate friends with Seattleites because its presence also cleaned up the tacky stretch of Pike Street above Fifth Avenue. The top four floors have their own lobby and offer a respite from the sometimes noisier lower floors. It has a now-famous restaurant named Fullers in honor of the family who supported the Seattle Art Museum for nearly half a century, and it has many Northwest artists represented on the walls. *Expensive.*

Sorrento Hotel, Ninth Avenue and Madison Street (206-622-6400). This quiet hotel is a brisk walk downtown (the walk back is up a very steep hill, so wear your running or walking shoes), but it is one of the most charming places in the city. That distance from the downtown core gives a bit of peace and quiet. Its views, particularly from the two enormous suites on the top floor, are unmatched by any other hotel in the city. Its Hunt Club Restaurant gets as many rave reviews as the hotel itself. *Expensive.*

Stouffer Madison Hotel, Sixth Avenue and Madison Street (206-583-0300). Seattleites like this luxury-class hotel because it is also one of the most unpretentious. It has an exterior that is just okay and a simple, open lobby, leaving the best for the rooms. They are equipped with handmade cabinets and easy-on-the-nerves decor, plus a gym, sauna, two restaurants, a 24-hour expresso bar and great urban and Sound views from most rooms. *Expensive.*

Travelodge Downtown, 2213 Eighth Ave. (206-624-6300). The motel has 72 units and is one of the scheduled stops for the Gray Line Quick Shuttle to the airport. *Moderate.*

Hotel Vintage Park, Fifth Avenue and Spring Street (206-624-8000 or 800-624-4433). This is one of the newest and most imaginative hotels with a staff trained to mingle with guests—the manager often goes on early-morning runs with guests. Each room is named for a Washington winery, and free wine and snacks are served each evening. *Expensive.*

The Warwick, Fourth Avenue and Lenora Street (206-443-4300). Just up the street from the Westin, and still within easy walking distance of the downtown core, this is a popular hotel for travelers, and you'll often see airline crews in the lobby. Exercise room, sauna, good city views from balconies. *Expensive.*

WestCoast Camlin Hotel, Ninth Avenue at Pine Street (206-682-0100). This smallish hotel was recently refurbished. It is conveniently located with excellent views over the skyline. Its top-floor Cloud Room Restaurant has one of the best views in town. *Moderate.*

Westin Hotel, Fifth Avenue and Westlake (206-728-1000). This twin-towered hotel is a wonderful place to go for lunch in the Market Cafe, or dinner in Nikko's, just a drink in the lobby or in Fitzgerald's, which looks like bars should look. Its rooms are more than adequate, unless you insist on squared-off corners in your life; the round towers prevent that. It has one of the best locations in Seattle, only a block or two from the best department stores. *Expensive.*

The Airport Strip

Comfort Inn at SeaTac, 19333 Pacific Highway S. (206-878-1100). A comfortable motel near a restaurant, close to the airport with good furnishings, an exercise room and a whirlpool. *Moderate.*

Holiday Inn of Sea-Tac, 17338 Pacific Highway S. (206-248-1000). This hotel is closer to the terminal than most and has all the amenities business travelers and vacationers will need. *Moderate.*

Marriott, 3201 S. 176th St. (206-241-2000). Like its twin brothers and sisters throughout the country, this is one of the more elaborate hotels near the airport. It has a wide selection of dining areas, a lobby large enough to hold a busload of customers and luggage without creating a traffic jam, and adequate rooms and meeting facilities. *Expensive.*

Radisson Hotel Seattle Airport, 17001 Pacific Highway S. (206-244-6000). This low-profile place, which began as a Hyatt, has been at the airport longer than most. Its nearly 300 units spread out horizontally rather than vertically and it is a popular place for banquets and conferences. Easy access to the airport. *Moderate.*

Red Lion Inn, Pacific Highway S. and 188th Avenue (206-246-8600). This gorilla of airport hotels dwarfs the others. It is so large that boxing matches are held in its banquet room. It has 850 rooms and glass elevators. (Remember when these were considered pretentious? Now they are being praised because they are safer for women traveling alone.) Two good restaurants, one on the top floor with views across the airport and mountain ranges. *Expensive.*

Sandstone Inn, 19225 Pacific Highway S. (206-824-1350). This modest but clean motel is popular with people who want to spend a night at the airport rather than rising in the middle of the night to drive there. Like many reasonably priced airport motels, the Sandstone has special prices for guests who park for several days. Restaurant. *Moderate.*

Bed and Breakfasts

Seattle has dozens of B&Bs and inns. Many guests use the following reservation services, although you should be aware that many do not accept single-night reservations:

Pacific Bed & Breakfast, 701 N.W. 60th St., Seattle, 98107. Phone: 206-784-0539.

Traveler's Bed & Breakfast, P.O. Box 492, Mercer Island, 98040. Phone: 206-232-2345.

RV Parks

If you arrive in your motorhome or camper you'll most likely have to stay on the outskirts of Seattle. These campgrounds are near Metro bus lines. Most are open the year around, but you should call before arriving.

Seattle South KOA, 5801 S. 212, Kent (206-872-8652), has 152 sites and is open all year. Laundry, grocery store, heated pool and playground are included.

Twin Cedars RV Park, 17826 Highway 99 N. (206-742-5540) is north of Seattle and has 68 sites, laundry and a recreation room.

SEATTLE RESTAURANTS

 When old-timers grumble about the changes that have occurred in Seattle since the 1962 World's Fair, they usually qualify their gripes by admitting that one of the good things about the New Seattle is the number of excellent restaurants. You can find almost any kind of food you want in a reasonable distance from your downtown hotel. All parts of Asia are represented now, not only in the International District, and you can find food from almost every country and ethnic group in Europe. Caribbean restaurants are doing well, as are North African and Latin American. This book can't possibly list all the good places to eat; I've left that for writers who specialize in food. It is best to check with your concierge or pick up a copy of the Friday edition of either the *Times* or the *Post-Intelligencer* for the entertainment tabloids published in each paper, or *The Weekly*.

Code: *Inexpensive – Under $10 per person; Moderate – $10 to $30; Expensive – Over $30.*

Adriatica, 1107 Dexter Ave. N. (206-285-5000). Specializing in eastern Mediterranean dishes, this restaurant is in a converted home on the west side of Lake Union with a great view across the lake and skyline. Its large menu includes dishes from Greece, Italy and the former Yugoslavia. It is frequently called one of the best regional and national restaurants, and was recently listed as one of the top 50 restaurants in the country by *Condé Nast Traveler. Expensive.*

Blue Star Café and Pub, 4512 Stone Way Ave. N. (206-548-0345). The first non-smoking pub in the area with some two dozen taps of local microbrews, cider and rootbeer. Sandwiches, salads, burgers, seafood and pastas. *Inexpensive.*

Campagne, Inn at the Market, 86 Pine St. (206-728-2800). Southern French cooking with Northwest ingredients is this expensive restaurant's specialty. Hours: Lunch, 11:30 A.M. – 2:30 P.M.; dinner, 5:30 – 11 P.M. daily.

Chandlers Crabhouse and Fresh Fish, 901 Fairview Ave. N. (206-223-2722). On the south shore of Lake Union at the foot of Fairview with views across the lake. Seafood, chicken and steaks. *Expensive.*

Elliott's , Pier 56 (206-623-4340). This top seafood restaurant on the waterfront specializes in crab, clams and freshly shucked oysters. Lunch and dinner daily. *Expensive.*

Georgian Room, Four Seasons Olympic Hotel, Fourth Avenue and University Street (206-621-7889). When the old Olympic Hotel was renovated into the Four Seasons Olympic, one result was this elegant dining room with a

Renaissance look and Northwest cuisine. Lunch, dinner and Sunday brunch. *Expensive.*

The Hunt Club, Sorrento Hotel, Ninth Avenue and Madison Street (206-622-6400). This popular, highly rated restaurant features a seasonal menu and a dress code. Open six days a week for lunch and dinner; Sunday brunches. *Expensive.*

Labuznik, 1924 First Ave. (206-441-8899). At one time this place was called The Prague and was one of Seattle's most popular restaurants. The owner, Peter Cipra, closed it and reopened as the Labuznik and it is as good or better than the predecessor. The menu remains intentionally small, but has wonderful Czech dishes such as svichova, sacher torte and Pala cinky. The restaurant in the rear is quiet and elegant; the café out front, which opens onto the street in good weather, is more informal and has a larger selection. Dinner: 4:30–10 P.M. Tues.–Thurs.; 5:30–midnight Fri. and Sat. Closed Sun. and Mon. *Moderate.*

McCormick's Fish House, 722 Fourth Ave. (206-682-3900). A highly rated seafood place popular with the after-work crowd, McCormick's is locally famous for its crab cakes, rock shrimp popcorn and steamed shellfish. *Moderate* to *Expensive.*

Metropolitan Grill, 818 Second Ave. (206-624-3287). The Metropolitan has made nearly every list of best places to eat in Seattle, including one of the top ten steak houses in America. As the name implies, steaks, chops and seafood are the specialties. *Expensive.*

The Painted Table, Alexis Hotel, First Avenue and Madison Street (206-624-3646). Here you'll find some of the best Northwest cuisine—seafood, produce and cheeses—but of equal interest are the plates you use. Each place has a hand-painted charger plate done by a Northwest artist, and you can buy the plate for $50 to $70, depending on the size. Lunch and dinner. *Moderate.*

Ray's Boathouse, 6049 Seaview Ave. N.W. (206-789-3770). This is probably the most popular seafood-with-a-view restaurant in the Puget Sound region. The place burned to the ground in 1987, and came back larger than before with chicken and beef added to the menu. Hours: lunch, 11:30 A.M.–2 P.M. Monday–Saturday; 10 A.M.–2 P.M. Sunday; dinner, 5–10 P.M. Sunday–Thursday; 5–10:30 P.M. Friday and Saturday. Valet parking. *Expensive.*

Salmon Bay Café, 5109 Shilshole Ave. N.W. (206-782-5539). If you're looking for the kind of place you might find commercial fishermen, boatbuilders and wharf rats with money under their Helly Hansen's, this is your kind of place. The breakfasts are enormous doses of chloresterol and sugar under the disguise of omelettes and cinnamon rolls. *Inexpensive.*

Salty's On Alki, 1936 Harbor Ave. S.W. (206-937-1600). Salty's has by far the best view of the Seattle skyline, and, unlike its predecessors, the food and service are up to the challenge. The menu is broadly based with a wide selection of salads, seafood, burgers and steaks. It is also a wonderful place to stop on a late winter afternoon to have a drink and watch the skyline gradually darken and the city lights come on. *Expensive.*

Space Needle, Seattle Center grounds. A new level has been added at the 100-foot level in the Needle called Wheedles. Open Memorial Day to Labor Day and mostly for tourists, it serves more simple fare than the restaurant on top. The top level gives you the 360-degree view of the region through its once-every-hour complete revolution. Elaborate menu. Lunch: Mon.–Sat. 11 A.M.–3 P.M. Dinner every day 4:30–10:30 P.M. Sunday brunch 10:30 A.M.–3 P.M. Reservations: 206-443-2100. Elevator costs $2 for adults, $1 for children. *Expensive.*

Wild Ginger, 1400 Western Ave. (206-623-4450). Local food critics have been raving about this place that specializes in Southeast Asian, Thai, Korean and hot Chinese dishes. Lunch is served Mon-Sat. Dinner: every night. *Moderate.*

View Restaurants

Although restaurants that advertise their "atmosphere" sometimes try to sell that instead of good food and service, still there is a demand for places to eat that have a view, especially for entertaining out-of-town guests. Here are a few listed according to what you will see:

City Skyline: Salty's, 1936 Harbor S.W.; The Cloud Room, Camlin Hotel, Eighth Avenue & Pine Street; The Space Needle, Seattle Center.

Lake Union: Arnie's, 1900 N. Northlake Way; Franco's Hidden Harbor, 1500 Westlake N.; Canlis, 2576 Aurora Ave. N.; Ivar's Salmon House, 401 N.E. Northlake Way; The Lakeside, 2501 Northlake Way.

Puget Sound & Olympics: Edgewater Inn, Pier 67; Elliott's Pier 56, The Galley, Pier 57; Hiram's at the Locks, 5300 34th Ave. N.W. (view of the locks); Quesnel's, 4703 Beach Dr. S.W.; Quinn's, Shilshole Bay; Ray's Boathouse, 6049 Seaview Ave. N.W.; Stuart's at Shilshole, 4135 Seaview Ave. N.W.

CULTURE

Galleries

The art gallery business is volatile. So many come and go that it is difficult to follow. However, Seattle has several that have been in business a long time and some of them are listed here. The major gallery event is the First Thursday gallery walk in Pioneer Square. The participating galleries—which is most of them—open their new shows on the first Thursday of each month, and the galleries stay open two or three hours, beginning at about 6 P.M. This popular event is a good way to see a lot of new art—and some interesting people—in a short time.

(Several galleries in Vancouver also have a First Thursday event.)

Arthead Gallery, 5411 Meridian Ave. N. (206-633-5544). Hand-printed limited edition prints by local artists are one of the gallery's specialties.

Artworks Gallery, 155 S. Main St. (206-625-0932). Gallery features porcelain, ceramics and glass pieces as well as paintings and prints.

Davidson Galleries, 313 Occidental Ave. S. (206-624-7684). Contemporary paintings, prints and drawings are featured with an emphasis on works on paper. Publishes posters and catalogs for national distribution.

Fireworks Gallery, 210 First Ave. S. (206-682-8707). As the name hints, only ceramics, glass and clay crafts are displayed.

Foster/White Gallery, 311 1/2 Occidental Ave. S. (206-622-2833). Specializes in contemporary Northwest ceramics, glass, paintings and sculpture.

Francine Seders Gallery, 6701 Greenwood Ave. N. (206-782-0355). Exhibitions of contemporary works with an emphasis on Northwest artists.

Gallery Mack, 2001 Western Ave., (206-448-1616). Lithographs, ceramics, paintings, posters and various other media are handled by this gallery.

Greg Kucera Gallery, 608 Second Ave. (206-624-0770). Fine arts gallery showing local and national artists.

Linda Hodges Gallery, 410 Occidental Ave. (206-624-3034). Works by regional and national artists.

Jackson Street Gallery, 163 S. Jackson St. (206-623-0435). Local and national artists are represented. Poetry readings and audio sculpture are sometimes featured.

Jacob Lawrence Gallery, University of Washington Art Bldg., Room 132. (206-685-1805). This gallery is devoted to the works of the famed painter and sculptor Jacob Lawrence, who is recognized as one of the United States' leading African American artists. Mr. Lawrence is also a member of the University's faculty.

Kirsten Gallery, 5320 Roosevelt Way N.E. (206-522-2011). A wide range of artistic styles are displayed: traditional, representational and abstract. The annual Northwest

Marine Art Exhibition in July and August is held here.

Linda Farris Gallery, 320 Second Ave. S. (206-623-1110). The gallery seeks museum-caliber work by regional and national artists.

Lisa Harris Gallery, 1922 Pike Place Market. (206-443-3315). Northwest and nationally known artists are presented, also limited edition lithographs, etchings, serigraphs, mezzotints and woodblock prints.

The Painted Table, Alexis Hotel, 92 Madison St. (206-624-3646). In addition to plates you can eat on and then buy, this unusual gallery/restaurant features a series of shows throughout the year.

Public Art Space, 305 Harrison St., Seattle Center House. (206-625-2216 or 625-4223). A collaborative gallery funded primarily by the Seattle and King County Arts commissions. The gallery displays new works from the collection bought by the city, county and state before they are installed elsewhere.

Runnings Gallery, 301 Occidental Ave. S. (206-682-8625). Represents local, national and international artists who work primarily in figurative art.

Snow Goose Gallery, 8806 Roosevelt Way N.E. (206-523-6223). Northwest Coast Indian and Inuit art. Shows display objects acquired on trips north by the owner, Jane Schuldberg.

Stonington Gallery, 2030 First Ave. (206-443-1108). Specializes in the work of contemporary Alaskan and Northwest artists with an emphasis on the cultures of Alaska. Limited-edition prints are a specialty.

Stroum Jewish Community Center, 3801 E. Mercer Way, Mercer Island (206-232-7115). Several exhibits by Jewish artists from all over the world are displayed at this popular center.

Museums

Seattle Art Museum, 100 University St. (206-654-3100). The new downtown $62 million museum, which opened in1991, has four floors of exhibit space to show off many of the museum's 18,500-piece collection.

The Museum Store is on the first floor, along with a 299-seat auditorium and The Restaurant, which serves hot and cold entrées in an outdoor-café setting. The mezzanine and second floor houses traveling exhibitions. The third floor displays the permanent collections of African, Northwest Coast Native American, Chinese, Japanese, Korean and Pre-Islam Persian collections. The fourth floor has Northwest "Old Masters," such as Mark Tobey and Morris Graves, photographs, and European collections from medieval times until the present.

Notable collections include that of Samuel H. Kress, which features a ceiling fresco by Giovanni Tiepolo and the Venus and Adonis by Paolo Caliari. The Norman Davis collection of Greek coins is one of the major such collections in the world. Perhaps the most impressive collection is the Oriental art left to the museum by the late Dr. Richard Fuller, the man who built the Volunteer Park Museum and gave it to the city.

The museum is closed Mondays, Thanksgiving (U.S.), Christmas and New Year's Day. Admission is free to members. The first Tuesday of each month is free day for everyone. No admission is charged for using the Museum Store or The Restaurant.

The former museum in Volunteer Park was renovated and reopened as **The Asian Art Museum** in 1993. Its exhibit space is devoted to the museum's enormous Asian collection. (206-654-3185)

Museum of Flight, 9404 E. Marginal Way S. (206-764-5720). This relatively new museum shows the history of flight with an emphasis on the West Coast and the Pacific Rim. Obviously The Boeing Company is well represented,

Following Pages:
Exhibits in the Museum of Flight's Great Gallery chronicle the history of flight.
DENNIS FLEISHMAN

including the Red Barn, which was Boeing's first aircraft plant. The Great Gallery displays more than 40 aircraft, many of which are suspended from the ceiling. The collection includes a 1929 Boeing Model 80A-1, an Apollo command module, a DC3, Corsair and numerous fighter planes. It also has a hands-on exhibit area for children. Hours: Daily 10 A.M. – 5 P.M.; Thursday until 9 P.M. Closed December 25. Admission.

Klondike Gold Rush National Historical Park, 117 S. Main St. (206-553-7220). When gold was discovered in the Klondike, Seattle became the launching pad for the last of the great stampedes for gold. The park/museum shows Seattle's role in outfitting miners and guiding them to the long trek to Dawson City, Yukon, during the 1897–98 event. Park rangers demonstrate gold-panning techniques and explain the ton of gear each miner had to take. Films, including Charlie Chaplin's *Gold Rush,* are shown in the auditorium. Open daily. Free.

Burke Museum, 17th Avenue N.E. and N.E. 45th Street, University of Washington Campus (206-543-7907). The Burke is nationally known for its collections in anthropology—particularly related to the Pacific—and geology and zoology. Northwest Coast Indian art is perhaps its best known collection. The museum sponsors many guided tours, lectures, field trips and traveling collections. It has a gift shop and "Boiserie" expresso cafe. Admission. Hours: Tues. – Fri. 11 A.M. – 5:30 P.M.; Sat. – Sun. 9 A.M. – 4:30 P.M.

Nordic Heritage Museum, 3014 N.W. 67th St. (206-789-5707). For generations Seattleites have joked about the Scandinavian influence while admiring many of the contributions to the region from Norway, Sweden and Denmark (and Finland, too, even though Finland isn't Scandinavian). One of the newer museums in Seattle, this one has an extensive permanent collection and a lively series of shows by Scandinavian artists from Europe and the Northwest.

Frye Art Museum, Terry Avenue and Cherry Street (206-622-9250). This small, low-key museum was given to the city by the late Charles and Emma Frye. It has an impressive permanent collection that includes works by Edouard Manet, Childe Hassam, Andrew Wyeth, Mary Cassatt and a number of other artists from the 19th and 20th centuries. The museum mounts several shows by regional artists and each year sponsors the Puget Sound Area Exhibition and provides cash for the prizes. Free. Closed only on Thanksgiving (U.S.) and Christmas.

Museum of History and Industry, 2161 E. Hamlin St. (206-324-1125). This large institution on Lake Washington houses the best collection of Seattle memorabilia in existence. It also has an excellent library for researchers. Among its artifacts are Boeing's B-1 seaplane that delivered air mail between Victoria and Seattle, the first international air-mail service; several antique automobiles, fire engines and perhaps the only remaining Seattle cable car, and tons of maritime artifacts. The photo collection shows Seattle's entire history, the maritime history of Puget Sound and the Inside Passage, and the history of The Boeing Company. The museum is open every day. Admission.

Wing Luke Asian Museum, 407 Seventh Ave. S. (206-623-5124). Created in honor of a popular Seattle city council-man who disappeared in 1965 when his small plane crashed in the Cascades, this museum has gradually grown to become a major voice for the International District. The collection includes artwork and artifacts related to the Asian-American experience in the region, and includes everything from herbal medicines to parasols and fans. Classes are given in brush painting, origami and Oriental culture. Closed Mondays. Admission.

Henry Art Gallery, 15th Ave. N.E. and N.E. 41st St. (206-543-2280) on the University of Washington campus. This popular museum is going through a major expansion program that will double its space when it is completed in 1996. It began as the state's first art museum in 1927 and its collection has increased steadily over the years. Its permanent collection includes Winslow Homer, William Merritt Chase and Mark Tobey. It is also well known for its textile and dress collection, the Monsen Study Collection of Photography and a large video collection. Closed major holidays. Admission.

Stage Theaters

Seattle has always been a good theater town, although nobody is quite sure how this came to be. Today the credit goes to the strong sense of community among the theater groups, who feel that their competition is other forms of entertainment rather than each other. This frees them to share equipment and facilities and marketing information to build the genre rather than remaining fragmented.

The city has about a dozen equity theaters and dozens of small experimental groups that may never get publicity beyond the neighborhood or the interest group that spawned them, so the following list makes no attempt to be complete. Check local papers for schedules.

A Contemporary Theater (ACT), 100 W. Roy St. (206-285-5110). One of Seattle's most successful equity theaters, it tries to present "the most important plays of our time."

Bathhouse Theater, 7312 W. Green Lake Dr. N. (206-524-9108). This popular, small theater presents five modern and classical plays the year around in its 130-seat theater on the northern edge of Green Lake.

The Cabaret, 111 Yesler Way (206-447-1514). This musical theater offers food and alcohol served by the cast in the European cabaret style.

Civic Light Opera, 11051 34th Ave. N.E. (206-363-2809). This popular group produces musicals in the Jane Addams Theater.

The Empty Space, 3509 Fremont Ave. N. (206-547-7500). An equity group specializing in new plays.

Evergreen Theater Conservatory, 1510 11th Ave. (206-328-8382). Semi-professional musicals and other productions are performed. Classes and workshops are offered.

The Foundation Theater, 7048 Earl Ave. N.W. (206-789-3241). The Commedia dell'arte and farce summer shows are produced at the Sylvan Outdoor Theater on the University of Washington campus.

The Group Theater Company, 3940 Brooklyn Ave. N.E. (206-441-1299). The resident group at The Ethnic Theater at University of Washington produces new scripts that deal with social problems in either a humorous or serious manner.

Intiman Theater Company, The Playhouse, Seattle Center (206-626-0782). A professional group that performs six plays each season from the library of international dramatic literature, both modern and classic.

Seattle Children's Theater, Seattle Center (206-441-3322). A professional group that produces five shows each year with a special holiday show in December. It performs in its own theater at Seattle Center and in the Poncho Theater at the south entrance of Woodland Park Zoo.

Seattle Gilbert & Sullivan Society (206-782-5466). A volunteer group that presents one G&S operetta each year in various locations.

Seattle Repertory Theater, 155 Mercer St. in the Bagley Wright Theater in Seattle Center (206-443-2222). Seattle's oldest equity theater produces six plays each year ranging from classic to modern, comedy to drama.

Musical Organizations

Seattle Symphony Orchestra, Opera House (206-443-4747). Under the direction of Gerard Schwarz, the SSO has become one of the best in the United States. Its repertoire includes the classics amd music by living composers. Concerts are given between October and April.

Seattle Opera Association, Opera House (206-389-7676). The opera made its mark in the 1970s by offering Wagner's complete Ring cycle in both German and English. It since outgrew the Ring and moved on to a mixture of standards, lesser-known works and new compositions. The season is from September to May.

Night Clubs

Rock is still king at night in Seattle, but you can also find clubs that feature blues, comedy and jazz, another Seattle staple.

For rock, try the **Crocodile Café,** 2200 Second Ave. (206-441-5611); the **Colourbox,** 113 First Ave. (206-340-4101); **Fenix Underground,** 323 Second Ave. S. (206-343-7740); **Off Ramp,** 109 Eastlake Ave. E. (206-628-0232) and the **Weathered Wall,** 1921 Fifth Ave. (206-448-5688).

For blues, try **Larry's,** 209 First Ave. S. (206-624-7665); **Under the Rail,** 2335 Fifth Ave. (206-448-1900), and the **Central Saloon,** 207 First Ave. (206-622-0209).

For jazz, **Jazz Alley,** 2033 Sixth Ave. (206-441-9729) and the **New Orleans Creole Restaurant,** 114 First Ave. S. (206-622-2563) are the best.

For comedy, try **Jet City Improv,** 115 Blanchard St. (206-781-3879); **Comedy Underground** at Swannie's, 222 S. Main St. (206-628-0303), and the **Seattle Improv,** 1426 First Ave. (206-628-5000).

*Peace Arch Park marks the >
international border between
the United States and Canada
at Blaine, Washington.*
ARCHIE SATTERFIELD

Between the
Cities

CHILDREN · OF · A · COMMON · MOTHER

When you travel between Seattle and Vancouver , you will probably want to give yourself enough time to stop in the smaller towns along the route, and to enjoy the pastoral scenery. Although the I-5 corridor is becoming distressingly crowded, you can still drive less than a mile from the freeway and be in the middle of vast farms, wildlife refuges and thick timber. Still, in spite of the problems with interstate driving, I-5 north of Seattle is one of the prettier interstates after you leave the city congestion.

Heading north from Seattle, you have several choices of routes. You can drive part of the way on I-5, then swing off to the west for a more leisurely and scenic drive up Whidbey Island, or swing over to the east and drive on Highway 9 along the edge of the Cascade Range. Or you can take the state's first designated scenic highway, Chuckanut Drive, which leaves I-5 just north of Mt. Vernon and follows the coast along the edge of mountains to Bellingham. You can then continue along the coastline from Bellingham to Birch Bay and rejoin I-5 just before crossing the border into British Columbia at Blaine.

One of my favorite routes is on **Whidbey Island.** Take the Mukilteo ferry across to Clinton on the southern tip of Whidbey Island, then drive its length and cross back to the mainland at Deception Pass. (See pages 77-80.) After leaving the island on Highway 20, a side trip to **La Conner** is worth taking. The former fishing town was discovered by a group of artists, who were in turn followed by gift shops. La Conner is a pleasant, if sometimes crowded, place to visit with good restaurants, some overlooking Swinomish Slough, the channel that separates Fidalgo Island from the mainland. Across the channel—over a graceful highway bridge that has won several awards— is the Swinomish Indian Reservation.

La Conner has a fine museum, **The Valley Museum of Northwest Art** (360-466-4288), in the Gaches Mansion at Second and Calhoun, where you can see work done by artists who live or once lived in the area. In spite of its sometimes oh-so-cute atmosphere, La Conner is still a working town with real commercial fishermen, a fish processing plant and a lot of farmers who raise bulbs and row crops.

If you are driving north from La Conner to catch Highway 20, you might consider going a short distance north to visit the **Padilla Bay National Estuarine Research Center,** 1043 Bay View-Edison Rd. (360-428-1558) in the community of Bay View. It is a 2,500-acre (1012-ha) reserve that covers marine waters, tideflats, marshes, beaches and uplands, and 3 miles (5 km) of trails. It has an interpretive center with photographs, dioramas and artifacts related to Padilla Bay, an aquarium and a library. The center is open Wednesday through Sunday. Free.

Mount Vernon is the hub of the broad, rich Skagit Valley, sometimes called Skagit Flats because the valley lies flat as a table. Here in the spring you'll see thousands of acres of tulips, daffodils and iris because the valley specializes in growing bulbs as well as seed crops, such as potatoes, onions, carrots and mustard. Mount Vernon has two or three good restaurants and one or two bed and breakfasts, but it isn't really a destination town. The town's big event is the Tulip Festival each April when thousands of acres of tulips are blooming in the fields west of town. The festival has several events, including a marathon, and thousands of visitors who clog the country roads. You'll be better off riding a bike or walking between the fields during this period.

Later in the spring you can see almost as many iris and daffodils in the fields, but it is the tulips that get the most attention. Information: Mount Vernon Chamber of Commerce (360-428-8547).

North of Mount Vernon on I-5—just past the factory outlet mall—you'll come to the turnoff to **Chuckanut Drive.** This was the state's first designated scenic drive and reminds everyone of parts of California's Highway 1. The route first goes across more of the Skagit Valley, then suddenly arrives at Chuckanut Mountain, where the most beautiful 7-mile (11-km) stretch begins. If you're driving a large motorhome or pulling a trailer, you may want to skip this route because the narrow road is often steep with sharp curves.

The drive clings to the side of steep mountains with several turnouts for views across the sound to Anacortes, the

Olympic Mountains, Vancouver Island and Victoria, and the San Juan Islands. Three good restaurants have been on the drive for many years. **Chuckanut Manor** (360-766-6191) is at the southern end, a farmhouse-style place that features smorgasbords and is always casual. It also has a guest room upstairs.

Next is the **Oyster Bar** (360-766-6185) that seems to cling to the sheer mountainside. It is very small, and the most expensive of the three. The third is the **Oyster Creek Inn** (360-766-6179) which is built onto the side of another cliff and is spread over two levels overlooking Oyster Creek. The drive also has an unusual bed and breakfast called the **Bay House**. It is a small cottage with Japanese furniture just down the road from Chuckanut Manor. It is stocked with champagne, dessert, and breakfast for you to cook yourself.

North of Oyster Creek Inn is **Larrabee State Park** on a picturesque, rocky cove with trails leading around the edge of rocky points and a gravely beach. And not much farther north you will pass one of the few nude beaches in Washington. Teddy Bear Cove (not marked on your AAA map, I assure you) is just north of Larrabee State Park. When you see a large cluster of cars parked beside the highway for no apparent reason, you'll know you're passing Teddy Bare Cove.

Chuckanut Drive ends in the Fairhaven district of **Bellingham,** which is the most beautiful part of the city. Its Victorian homes and stores were built on the western and northern edge of steep hills, which gives it stunning views across the saltwater to Vancouver Island. Fairhaven has several restaurants and coffee shops, and one of the best bookstores in the region, Village Books.

The **Whatcom Museum of History and Art,** 121 Prospect St. (206-676-6981) is a superb museum with changing exhibits of regional art and major historical collections.

On the northern edge of town is the relatively new shopping mall, **Bellis Fair.** It has at least five major department stores, more than 120 small shops and a six-screen movie theater. Just across the street are the Meridian Plaza, Meridian Village and Cordata Place, all smaller shopping centers.

These malls are there mainly for Canadian shoppers, who come south of the border for better prices. Taxes are much higher in Canada, in part because Canada provides better services for its citizens than does the American government. An unfortunate consequence is that Canadian merchants lose customers to the merchants in Washington. Many items are still cheaper when bought in the U.S., even after paying duty and sales tax. Gasoline and cigarettes are among the products that are considerably cheaper.

This disparity in prices—Canada, like European countries, charges the actual price of producing its gasoline and diesel rather than subsidizing the industry—has made a tiny speck of the United States one of the oddest places on the continent: **Point Roberts.** This 5-square-mile (12.9-km^2) peninsula near the Tsawwassen ferry terminal was created when Kaiser Wilhelm ordained that the international boundary be on the 49th Parallel, with some zigging and zagging among the archipelago of islands. The British were aware that this appendix hung south of the 49th Parallel, and some suggested making a deal with the Americans to claim it, but nothing came of it until it was too late.

Thus, a small enclave of the United States hangs down from Canada, creating both obstacles and opportunities. Among the obstacles are that school children must be bussed more than 30 miles (48 km) each way to school in Blaine. The opportunities are that merchants can make fortunes selling goods to Canadians that are cheaper than across the border. Gasoline trucks make regular runs to the service stations. Grocery stores abound, and until British Columbia relaxed its laws on adult films, theaters showing X-rated films at both Blaine and Point Roberts were filled.

Point Roberts isn't much of a town. It has an enormous boat basin, a scattering of homes and the row of businesses along the main drag just below the border crossing. And the post office; it takes mail so long to be delivered from one country to the other that Canadians who do business in the States rent post office boxes in the border towns. The border is marked by a swath cut through the timber, as it is all the way across the continent. Few pay much attention to

it. Locals walk back and forth across it and nobody particularly cares even though it is illegal.

One of the strangest border incidents involving the two countries occurred at Point Roberts many years ago. An American hired a Canadian building contractor to do some clearing and grading work for him with his bulldozer. Then the American refused to pay. After repeated billings, bad words and threats, the Canadian had had enough. He cranked up his bulldozer, drove it across the border and proceeded to thoroughly demolish the work he had done

∧ *A tour boat out of Bellingham stops to watch a pod of orcas.*
Bellingham/Whatcom County Convention and Visitors Bureau

for the American. The American got very upset and got his gun. The Canadian beat a gleeful retreat, as hasty as a Caterpillar tractor will permit, and clattered across the border in a hail of rifle bullets. The last I heard, the authorities never got around to charging the Canadian with unlawful trespass or whatever.

Back to I-5: It is a straight run from Bellingham to the I-5/Highway 99 border crossing at Blaine/Douglas. Most people take this main route, but a few turn off at Bellingham and go up a highway that in Washington is called Guide Meridian, but is numbered Highway 539. In British Columbia it is shown on maps as the Aldergrove-Bellingham Highway. It doesn't go through any towns but skirts

Lynden, a dairy-farming town only 3 miles (4 km) from the border. **Lynden** has an unusual entrance off the main drag; you drive through the cemetery. Lynden's residents are predominately of Dutch extraction, so recently the buildings of Lynden were remodeled to give them a Dutch appearance. A shopping center was built with that theme, and a hotel in the downtown district is inside an enormous windmill. Information: Lynden Chamber of Commerce, 360-354-5995.

Another route from Bellingham runs along the beach at **Birch Bay** to Semiahmoo and on to Blaine. Birch Bay is a broad bay so shallow you can walk out for perhaps half a mile at low tide. The beach is one of the best in the region and you'll see volleyball nets strung on it between tides. The town has an amusement park and one of the most heavily policed main drags in the Evergreen Triangle. Consequently, the town is kept safe for kids and pets and is dedicated to summer homes, condominiums and service people. Information: Chamber of Commerce, 360-371-7675.

The road curves around the broad bay, then turns north along the low-bank coastline to **Semiahmoo,** the large resort on Drayton Harbor at Blaine. In the early years of this century Semiahmoo was the largest salmon cannery in the world. It was owned by Alaska Packing Association, a consortium of canneries who banded together rather than compete in a dying industry. The APA owned the Star Fleet, a fleet of beautiful sailing ships all named the Star of something. The only one remaining is the *Star of India*, berthed in San Diego's harbor. After the salmon declined, Alaska Packing Association pulled out and the buildings went into decline before the site was bought for a resort. In addition to the hotel, restaurants (and very good ones they are), the condominium and housing development, the resort has a world-class golf course. Information: 206-371-2000.

If you stay on I-5, you might consider taking a side trip at **Ferndale** to break up the white-knuckled, clenched-teeth aspects of freeway driving. Ferndale is a pleasant farm town that has a 1950s look to it, and two unusual county parks. **Pioneer Park** (360-384-5113), two blocks south of

Main Street on First Avenue, was created by saving log cabins, 10 of them, that were built by pioneers. One was a hotel, another was a granary and the rest were homes. Each is filled with artifacts from the pioneer period. Free.

The other park/museum is **Hovander Homestead Park** (206-384-3444) on Nielsen Road near Ferndale. It is an entire working farm that was donated to Whatcom County, and is a National Historic Site. It has a large, authentically furnished farmhouse where docents cook meals on the woodstove in the kitchen, an enormous red barn, farm animals and crops that are cultivated and harvested on antique equipment. Free tours in the summer.

Blaine is next and I hope you will excuse my frequent references to the friendship between Canada and the U.S. After having traveled throughout much of the world and seen what has happened when national neighbors don't get along in places like the former Yugoslavia, the Sudan, Jordan and Europe, it becomes apparent how fragile national boundaries and friendships really can be.

Thus, every time I drive across the border at Blaine/Douglas, even though the lines may be long and the weather miserable, I feel better about one part of the world when I look at the **Peace Arch**. This large arch in a broad, well manicured lawn has two slogans on it. Facing the American side are the words, "Children of a common mother," and facing Canada are the words, "Brethren dwelling together in unity."

The arch and the park was a project of a wealthy, energetic and very patriotic American industrialist named Samuel Hill. He married more wealth when he wed the daughter of railroad magnate James J. Hill, thus saving her the necessity of learning a new name. Hill worked on several civic projects throughout the Pacific Northwest, including underwriting part of the original Columbia River Highway. He got the idea for the Peace Arch and enlisted the help of school children to raise funds for the park.

The park is a pleasant no-man's land where people from both countries wander around freely for picnics and strolls. It is a gathering place for the peace lobby, and each June the arch is celebrated by the International Peace Arch Association.

Inside the columns of the arch are metal containers that hold pieces of the *Mayflower*—the American Pilgrims' ship—and the *Beaver,* Canada's first steam vessel on the West Coast.

Just north of the border, on the north side of Boundary Bay, is **White Rock,** a beach town without the resort atmosphere. For decades it has been a favored place for Vancouverites to build summer homes, and more recently it has become a mecca for retirees from all across Canada, and as such remains primarily residential.

Before you go to downtown Vancouver, you might want to take a brief side trip, or perhaps even stay overnight, at a charming little town at the end of the road that is also a good place to stop for a hostess gift if you're going to friends for dinner.

Until recently **Steveston** was a small fishing village at the mouth of the Fraser River that had an unplanned, unaffected charm. It still looks like what it has always been—a small fishing village at the end of the road—but it has been "discovered" and is becoming a popular, slightly rural experience for Vancouverites.

Locals like to remind visitors that the town is still very much a working town and that they intend to keep it that way, while increasing their income from tourism. Its commercial fishing heritage is being preserved in the Gulf of Georgia Building at the foot of Fourth Avenue. Built in 1894, the cannery has been designated a Federal Heritage Site, and the Canadian Park Service has begun work that will turn it into the West Coast Fishing Industry Museum with antique working cannery equipment.

The tourist industry was started by fishermen selling fresh seafood off their boats—salmon, shrimp, cod, halibut, tuna, prawns and crab. Even without the fish sales, Steveston's charm assures its place as a tourist destination. In addition to the hundreds of commercial fishing boats and their colorful nets hung out for repairs, Steveston has several cafés, a scattering of antique shops and several clothing stores.

One of the most picturesque buildings is the small two-story, frame 1906 Northern Bank Building on Moncton

Street that houses both the Steveston Historical Society museum and the post office. The nearby Cannery Café occupies a former cannery bunkhouse. Most of the business district occupies about four blocks of Moncton Street with a few stores on Bayview Street overlooking the fishing fleet at Steveston Landing. The town is so compact that it is ideal for walking and bicycling.

Garry Point Park stretches westward to saltwater from the edge of town. Originally the point was a dumping ground for dredges that scoured silt from the Fraser River shipping channel, but the park was created after the point had grown several feet above flood stage. It became a broad expanse of trails, mounds, picnic tables, open space and a lagoon where children can splash about and go fishing. Kite clubs gather there during the summer, and bagpipe players often salute the end of the day.

Garry Point Park connects with a series of trails atop dikes that go most of the way around Lulu Island, a large, low island between the two arms of the Fraser River. The trail leads north from Steveston along the coast and past marshes where migratory waterfowl and songbirds can be seen and on to the narrow channel separating the island from the Vancouver International Airport. A southern route follows dikes along the Fraser River and past dairy farms, boatyards and open fields. Canoeing and kayaking are also popular in the marshes and sloughs of the Fraser River delta.

Steveston is 4 miles (6.5 km) west of Highway 99 on the Steveston Highway, which exits at the first intersection north of the George Massey Tunnel.

The usual route for visitors to Vancouver is on Highway 99 right into the heart of the city. The highway goes through the George Massey Tunnel, beneath the south arm of the Fraser River, across Lulu Island and through Richmond, which is the gateway to the Vancouver International Airport, then over the Oak Street bridge and into the city limits. Or you can stay on Oak Street to Broadway, turn left to Granville and right on Granville across the Granville Bridge and into the downtown area.

A better route is to take the second right at the end of the

Oak Street bridge, which puts you briefly on S.E. Marine Drive. Follow it a short distance west to Granville Street, which takes you north into the city.

Sometimes for variety and different scenery, I take Highway 99A, also known as the King George Highway, at the first major interchange north of the border. This takes you into downtown New Westminster, where you can stop at the waterfront complex with the public market and boat displays, described on page 109. After leaving New Westminster, Highway 99A becomes Kingsway and enters downtown Vancouver around the east end of False Creek.

GETTING AROUND THE ISLANDS

 One of the greatest pleasures of traveling in the Evergreen Triangle is visiting the great archipelago of islands between the three major cities. More than any other place in the Evergreen Triangle, these islands give you a feeling of being in a foreign country. They look almost identical—after all, they are only a short distance offshore—yet when the ferries pull away from the dock in Anacortes, Washington, or Sidney, B.C., you can almost hear a collective sigh of relief among the passengers, who by departure time have lined the decks and windows to wave goodbye to the mainland.

British Columbia has the largest fleet of vehicle-passenger ferries in North America, and Washington has the largest fleet in the United States. If anything is a symbol of this protected waterway, it has to be those awkward-looking, open-ended ferries with a strange, gawky grace. Next to having your own boat, they are the best way to see the saltwater of the Evergreen Triangle.

Ferries will take you to four of the San Juan Islands, and to the urbanized Bainbridge Island and the stubbornly rural Vashon Island. They will take you to and from Victoria, North Vancouver, Nanaimo and Tsawwassen. They are your means of driving to the beautiful Gulf Islands and they will get you to individual islands, such as Guemes and Lummi and Whidbey. They form moving bridges that you will share with semi-trucks, delivery vans, passenger buses, bicycles, walk-on passengers and groups of twittering school children. You will share the seats with snoozing stockbrokers and eager birders with binoculars and long-lensed cameras. The B.C. Ferries, Washington State Ferries, various provincial, county and privately owned ferries and the lines of vehicles waiting on long weekends, too, are a part of the Evergreen Triangle mystique.

Ferries provide entertainment for travelers, sometimes intentionally, sometimes not. Occasionally a confused passenger will drive right off the end of the ferry for no known reason. Sometimes you will see mountain climbers crawling "up" a wall by rapelling themselves along in the ferry parking lanes, pretending they are climbing when they actually are crawling across the pavement. That is only one of the cultural activities you can expect to see while waiting for the ferry. You will sometimes see people who wait until the last possible moment before leaping aboard, and you might (or might not) be surprised what people do in cars while waiting for ferries.

Each ferry has an observation deck and food service that ranges from the elaborate on the British Columbia fleet with its uniformed waiters to the fast-food counters on the short runs between Puget Sound islands and the mainland. Ferries provide the most direct route to the hiking, fishing and sightseeing on Vancouver Island and the Olympic Peninsula, to the historic towns of Port Townsend and Port Gamble, and to all the resorts along Hood Canal, Puget Sound, the Gulf Islands and the Strait of Juan de Fuca.

Unfortunately, international travel regulations do not permit direct ferry dockings between the San Juan Islands of Washington and the Gulf Islands of British Columbia. From Washington you must drive to Tsawwassen, south of Vancouver, or Horseshoe Bay, north of Vancouver, to reach the Gulf Islands of Canada; or cross to Victoria from Port Angeles or to Sidney on Vancouver Island from Anacortes, then catch a B.C. ferry. In British Columbia you must catch the Washington State Ferry at Sidney on Vancouver Island to reach the San Juan Islands.

While each of the three cities has its own distinct personality, you'll be surprised at how many of these islands also have their own personalities in terms of physical appear-

ance, activities available, and in terms of the kind of people who live on them. Some will remind you of a golf-and-country club, others have remnants of the hippie era, and others will be almost entirely rural with second and third-generation farmers and ranchers working the land.

Beginning in Puget Sound and working north into British Columbian waters, more than 100 islands appear on American charts and of these perhaps 20 have permanent residents. This does not include the more urban islands near Seattle, such as Bainbridge and Vashon. Whidbey, the largest of them all, is discussed below.

They form an enormous maze of islands that runs from the southern tip of Puget Sound all the way north through the Inside Passage of British Columbia and Southeast Alaska. They have always been remote, and the residents want them to remain so. You must want to visit them in order to see them; they're not on your way somewhere else. And while they're too far offshore to seriously consider building bridges to link them with the mainland, you can be sure such a plan would cause the residents to stage a rebellion.

One of Port Townsend's restored ∧
Victorian mansions, many of
which are bed-and-breakfasts.
Washington State Travel

Whidbey Island: Elegance in a Rural Setting

When the United States Supreme Court ruled in 1985 that Long Island, New York, was actually a peninsula because the East River that separates it from the mainland is fresh rather than saltwater, nobody was more surprised and pleased than the residents of Whidbey Island. Their island isn't long—only 40-odd miles (64 km) compared with Long Island's 118 miles (189 km)—but that is enough to make it the longest island in the 48 contiguous states. Small by British Columbian and Alaskan standards, but sufficient for local boasting.

The island is one of those places that invites use of the word "motoring" rather than simply going for a drive. It is convenient to the cities along Interstate 5 but still largely rural. It has a good north-south highway and pleasant country roads. In recent years the island has become more and more popular due to the natural beauty its residents protect so jealously. The mainland is never far away, but Whidbey has that sense of remoteness you expect on islands. Almost as a bonus, it has a pair of storybook historic towns and a growing number of casually elegant bed-and-breakfast establishments. Add to this an unusual National Park, two rhododendron preserves and the most dramatic and popular park in the state park system and it is easy to understand why Northwesterners like Whidbey so much.

Although the island is hilly—ask any bicyclist—there are stretches of flatland with broad beaches and tons of driftwood piled around conveniently for beach fires. The coastline alternates between beaches, high banks and rocky bluffs.

To reach the island from the I-5 corridor, take the **Mukilteo ferry** for a 20-minute ride to Clinton, which is hardly more than a ferry landing with the obligatory restaurant and bar at the foot of a steep hill. Highway 525 runs the 60-mile (96-km) length of the island as it follows the contours of the land. The best scenery and both of the historic towns are off the main route, which gives you an excuse to follow the shoreline on winding blacktop roads.

Langley, perched on a high bluff overlooking Saratoga Passage and Camano Island toward the southern end of Whidbey, is one of those small false-front towns that looks as if it might have been trucked there by the set designer for a western film set in the Northwest rain forest. It has several nice shops, a historic false-front tavern and the Inn at Langley—probably the most expensive hotel on the island.

North a short distance, roughly in the middle of the island, is **Coupeville,** an old village clinging to a low bank above Penn Cove. Some of its buildings hang out over the cove on stilts. The new **Island County Historical Society Museum** stands on the edge of town and has an excellent collection of Indian baskets. Next door is one of the four remaining blockhouses built in Coupeville during the "Indian troubles" of 1855 when tribes all around the region were resisting the treaties being forced upon them by the territorial governor.

This strong sense of history on the island resulted in the creation of **Ebey's Landing National Historical Reserve,** one of the first such reserves in the nation designed to "preserve and protect a rural community which provides an unbroken historic record from the nineteenth century exploration and settlement in Puget Sound to the present time."

Whidbey is well known for its handcrafted products from a variety of cottage industries and its berries (until only recently the largest loganberry farm in America was on the island), so you will find all manner of local products to take home with you, ranging from woolen sweaters to jams, jellies and liqueurs.

At almost exactly the halfway point of the island is **Fort Casey State Park,** on a small hill overlooking the Strait of Juan De Fuca. This fort was one of the three that constituted the "Iron Triangle," which guarded the entrance of Puget Sound against invasion. Military buffs will enjoy looking at the old cannons installed there. They are called ten-inch disappearing rifles because when they were fired, the recoil would cause them to swing backward and down to be reloaded. They obviously were not the best weapon invented in America.

At the edge of the state park, the **Keystone ferry** runs back and forth to Port Townsend about every 45 minutes. You can give yourself a nice break in exploring Whidbey Island by parking your car in the big lot, buying a walk-on ferry ticket for the half-hour trip and spending an hour or two walking around the Victorian Port Townsend.

Washington's state flower is the rhododendron and Whidbey Island has excellent growing conditions for the flowering bush. The island has two "rhody" preserves. **Rhododendron State Park** is near Coupeville—not far from the town dump as a matter of fact—and here you will see rhododendrons up to 12 feet (3.7 m) tall along the circular drive through the small park.

The Seattle Rhododendron Society's 53-acre (21-ha) **Meerkerk Gardens** lie toward the southern end of the island just outside Freeland. The society is continually conducting experiments in hybridization, and during the blooming season in spring and early summer, you will see many colors of the beautiful flower.

The island's largest town is **Oak Harbor** with a population of around 10,000. It has a slight Dutch atmosphere from its original settlers, and some visitor facilities. Most of its income is from a Naval Air Station nearby.

Some of the best scenery comes last. At the very northern end of the island is **Deception Pass,** a narrow, churning, whirlpool-filled passage between Whidbey and Fidalgo Islands. Fidalgo has none of the island atmosphere because it is separated from the mainland only by short bridges.

Deception Pass State Park is the most popular park in the state's system. The drama of watching boats roaring full-throttle through the passage when the tide is changing, and being brought almost to a standstill, always makes for a bit of excitement, both aboard the boat and for those watching from the high bridges above the two channels.

Several small beaches are in the park, which means you will have a wide selection for picnics. The park has two freshwater lakes. No motors are allowed on Pass Lake, which is popular with fishermen. Overnight camping is available at two or three locations, but no lodging or restaurant facilities are within the park boundaries.

From the north end of the island, you can continue on to the San Juan Islands via the ferry from Anacortes, which is only a short distance away, or you can take Highway 20 east to Interstate 5.

For information on the more than 30 B&Bs and inns on the island, write to the Whidbey Island Bed and Breakfast Association, P.O. Box 259, Langley, WA 98260. Phone: 360-321-6272. For general information: Whidbey Chamber of Commerce, P.O. Box 52, Coupeville, WA 98239. Phone: 360-678-5434.

The San Juan Islands

Traveling in the San Juan Islands during the summer tourist season requires patience and tolerance. When traffic volume is high, ferries seldom operate on time. They may leave Anacortes on time at the start of the day, but before dark everything is off by an hour or two. Also, because the enormous ferries are double-ended, some-

Orcas: Mascot of the Evergreen Triangle

Residents love to joke about the plants and creatures of the region, and some say banana slugs or geoducks should be the official mascot. For the newcomer, banana slugs are enormous in terms of snails without shells, and geoducks are a subspecies of clams that are also very, very large.

Of all the Evergreen Triangle critters, killer whales probably com-mand the most love from the most people. They are a highly social animal; they live in family groups, or pods, and they never harm man. They may anger fishermen because they eat so many salmon —up to 250 lbs. (113 kg) a day—and when they are present, salmon beat a hasty retreat. But gener-ally the black and white brutes, which look a little like a two-toned 1955 Chevrolet, are a welcome addition to the protected waters.

times you will have to back your car onto them because it is the only practical way to load. Consider it part of the adventure.

The **Washington State Ferries** leave for the San Juans from the landing a short distance west of Anacortes and call on four of the islands: Lopez, Shaw, Orcas and San Juan. One of these ferries makes a round trip each day to Sidney, British Columbia. This international run leaves Anacortes at about 8 A.M. and arrives in Sidney about three hours later.

Approximate crossing times are: Anacortes to Lopez, 1 hour; Lopez to Shaw, 20 minutes; Shaw to Orcas, 10 minutes; Orcas to San Juan Island (Friday Harbor), 50 minutes.

Some ferry service is offered between the lesser-used islands. A county-owned ferry operates between downtown Anacortes and Guemes Island, a 10-minute trip. Guemes is one of those with virtually no visitor services,

Researchers have identified three main pods of orcas in the region for a total of about 80 animals. They spend their entire lives of up to 100 years with the matriarchal group they are born into.

Puget Sound and the Strait of Georgia are two of the few places in the world where they live in such harmony so close to humans. Like their cousins, the whales, they communicate by songs. Recordings show that the pods tend to have a favorite song they sing (or grunt and bark and whistle) over and over with variations that would make Bach or Brubeck pay attention.

Although now strictly protected by federal law, they weren't always. In the 1960s several were captured along the coast of British Columbia and kept in captivity in aquariums where they were taught to perform various tricks. Many are still in captivity, but no new ones will be added.

only a small grocery store and a modest park, which is the way residents like it.

Privately owned ferries and barges serve the other San Juan Islands, but not on a scheduled basis. Airplanes are the most popular form of transportation, and San Juan Airlines operates scheduled flights to the larger islands not served by the ferry system. These include Decatur, Waldron, Cypress, Blakeley and Stuart.

Some islands that are not on the ferry schedule are heavily populated, such as Blakely, Decatur and Waldron, but the residents are perfectly content using airplanes and boats for transportation; it they weren't, they'd move to one of the four with ferry access. None of these, it should be noted, has visitor facilities. Lodging and other services are found only on the islands where the ferries stop: Lopez, Shaw, Orcas and San Juan.

An increasing number of tour boats are making daily trips between the mainland and the islands during the summers. Gray Line offers daily trips from Bellingham to some of the islands as does Victoria Clipper of Seattle. Other boats operate out of Port Townsend. Check with the local chamber of commerce for information.

Although some of the islands are not much farther than shouting distance apart, each island has its own character and each attracts a different kind of resident. **Lopez** is stubbornly rural, and almost every attempt to "improve" it with housing developments, condominiums and planned neighborhoods has been soundly defeated. Because it has fewer hills than the others and less traffic, it is very popular with bicycle riders.

Lopez does have one modest resort, the Islander Lopez on Fisherman Bay. The island also has a scattering of country inns, such as **Mackaye** (pronounced "Mackie") **Harbor Inn**, known for its excellent food, and **Betty's Country Inn** near the ferry landing.

Shaw Island is hardly developed at all. Quiet and rural with no hotels, inns or restaurants, it has a country store and that is about all except for a handful of modest campgrounds and harbors for small boats.

Orcas Island is by far the largest of the group and probably the most popular with visitors because of its many resorts, inns, and public parks and campgrounds. It is shaped like a giant saddlebag with a long fjord called East Sound almost cutting it in half.

Mt. Constitution on Orcas is the highest mountain in the islands. It rises 2,400 feet (732 m) almost directly out of the ocean and is the centerpiece of 4,700-acre (1900-ha) **Moran State Park.** The park has nearly 200 camp-sites, a large freshwater lake and several hundred miles of hiking trails. A paved road climbs to the summit of Mt. Constitution where you will find great views—between radio and television antennas. You can see British Colum-bia, the Cascade Range and Mt. Baker to the east and the Olympic Mountains to the southwest.

The park is part of an estate owned by a shipbuilder and one-time Seattle mayor named Moran. His home was a mansion in the wilderness, constructed of odds and ends from ships built in his yard. After his death it was turned into **Rosario Resort,** the most elaborate in the islands. It has meeting rooms, a conference center, condominium units, a restaurant and a gymnasium. All are dominated by the portholes, brass railings, lanterns and other nautical equip-ment Moran had built into the main building.

Orcas also has a number of B&Bs, country inns and small hotels. The most striking, because of its location, is the **Orcas Hotel,** the first building you see on the hill just above the ferry landing. The old hotel was in such sad shape a few years ago that it was almost demolished, but a local group banded together to restore it and get it on the Regis-tered Historic Places list. Most of the dozen rooms have shared baths, except for third floor rooms which have indi-vidual baths. The hotel's restaurant and bar are popular places to wait for the ferry.

Another popular country inn, **Turtleback Farm Inn,** is in the middle of the island with peaceful views across the woods and meadows. It was built by Bill and Susan Fletcher. The daughter of the late athlete and actor Buster Crabbe, Susan jokes that she gave up the life of a pampered California socialite and moved to a remote island to cook for a dozen people at a time and to scrub floors and toilets.

Orcas Island's main business center is Eastsound, at the tip of the sound of the same name. Here you will find restaurants and hotels, gift shops, a lumber yard and the library.

San Juan Island's only town is Friday Harbor, the largest town in the islands and the county seat of San Juan County. More business is conducted here than in the other island towns combined, so Friday Harbor has more amenities, including several very good cafés and restaurants, one or two nice country-style inns and many rental condominiums.

If you are going to Friday Harbor's increasingly popular jazz festival held each July, it is best to leave your car at the Anacortes dock and go as a walk-on passenger or with your bicycle. Not only is it cheaper but thousands of people attend the festival, and cars are a bother because of the long ferry line and the impossibility of finding a place to park.

Most points of interest to visitors are on other parts of the island, such as the two-part **San Juan Island National Historic Park.** The park commemorates the event that led

The War with a Single Casualty

The Pig War incident occurred in 1859, after many years of an often uneasy joint occupancy by the Americans and British. Neither nation had established clear legal ownership of the islands, although the British had clearly been there first. The international boundary between Canada and the United States had been established along the 49th Parallel by the 1846 treaty. The treaty made ownership clear across the continent on solid ground, but what about the islands? Vancouver Island drops far below the 49th Parallel, as do all the islands. The question of this boundary was left up in the air.

As they had in the Oregon Territory, Americans kept coming to the islands, cutting down the trees, planting crops and building fences. With the

to the establishment of the international boundary along the 49th Parallel, a line the British felt was unfairly generous to the Americans. The park is divided into two camps because of the almost-war between American and English settlers over the death of a pig.

The visible legacy of the Pig War is a beautiful spot toward the northern end of San Juan Island and a more mundane, inhospitable spot on the southern end. The story is commemorated by the San Juan Island National Historic Park, which includes the opposing army installations: English and American Camps. English Camp is the more beautiful by far, located on a small, tree-lined cove with the blockhouse and barracks nicely framed by enormous trees. It is often used for small festivals and similar public gatherings.

Little is left of American Camp, down on the windswept, treeless southern end of San Juan Island. It is known mostly for the infestation of rabbits that have turned the park into a maze of burrows. The rabbits were brought to the island

unquestionable wisdom of hindsight, we can now see that a showdown was inevitable. It was a situation that had to reach a crisis before it could be resolved.

The acrimony between the two nations came to a head when an American from Ohio named Lyman Cutler killed a pig that had been rooting up his garden. The pig belonged to the local Hudson's Bay agent named Charles J. Griffin, and Cutler had

asked Griffin repeatedly to keep his animals off Cutler's land. Griffin thought that was a bit cheeky considering that the Hudson's Bay Company had been there long before Cutler and his Indian wife arrived.

One morning in 1859 Cutler reached the end of his patience. He heard a pig rooting around in his garden, got out his Kentucky rifle and shot the pig dead. He saddled up his horse and rode over ➤

decades ago. Some got away and did what rabbits do. Without natural enemies on the island to keep them in balance, they have multiplied and multiplied beyond the point of control.

On the far northern end of San Juan Island is **Roche Harbor,** one of the most attractive resorts in the Northwest. It includes the historic frame Hotel DeHaro (where President Teddy Roosevelt slept) and a restaurant right on the water. Having breakfast in the restaurant will remind you of the nicer mornings in life. The night I spent in the aging hotel with slanting floors reminded me of cheap hotels I stayed in while working as a ranch hand in Wyoming and Colorado. But the woman I was with loved the place. Roche Harbor was once a lime factory owned by an eccentric named John S. McMillin, who built a mansion and an enormous mausoleum for himself that he called Afterglow Vista, which still stands. Several of the workers' cottages were restored and are rented to families and groups. Roche Harbor is a popular place for boaters, especially mainlanders who, I

to Griffin's home, told him what he had done and offered to replace it. Griffin was enraged and refused the offer. Thus, the Pig War of San Juan Island began and continued through the American Civil War years.

Both nations sent troops to the island. The English camped on the northern end in a beautiful cove, while the Americans chose an open, barren and windy spot at the southern end.

Although there was a lot of bluster and musket-rattling, not much really happened. No shots were fired (other than the one that killed the pig in the first place), but the "war" didn't end until 1871, when the German emperor, Kaiser Wilhelm, was asked to determine the line through the islands.

The British wanted all of the San Juan Islands, and were willing to leave Lummi, Cypress, Fidalgo am told, come over from Bellingham and Victoria to party late into the night.

The most popular spectator sport for visitors to San Juan Island is standing on the cliffs on the west side watching killer whales (orcas) cruise up and down the archipelago. These two-toned whales are so beloved in the area that one of Friday Harbor's most popular attractions is the **Whale Museum** in the heart of town.

Most people agree that the best time to visit the islands is in the off-season, even in the dead of winter when you can walk on the beach without seeing another person.

For information on the San Juans, contact the San Juan Islands Tourism Cooperative, P.O. Box 65, Lopez, WA 98261. Phone: 360-468-3663. For information on B&Bs: 360-378-3030.

Lummi Island is technically part of the San Juans and is served by a ferry from the mainland near Bellingham. The ferry leaves from a dock from the Lummi Indian Reservation near the Lummi Casino, one of three or four casinos

and Whidbey islands to the Americans. One compromise floated would have given the British San Juan, Waldron and Stuart islands. The Americans wanted exactly what they got, the boundary as it exists today; it looks like a jigsaw puzzle.

The islands have remained a frequent source of irritation between the two countries, sometimes because a Customs Inspector decides to enforce a particularly obscure law and seizes a Canadian's boat or personal belongings. It is enough to convince you that bureaucrats of both countries have little time bombs in their brows that go off every decade or two, reminding them that it is time to go forth and annoy thy neighbor.

operating on Indian reservations in Washington. The casino is open 24 hours a day. Information: 1-800-776-1337.

Lummi Island, which is not part of the reservation, is still only slightly developed in spite of being only about ten miles from Bellingham and a ten-minute ferry ride. It has a single store, a small community center, a café, and three bed-and-breakfasts: The **Willows Inn** (360-758-2620); West Shore Farm (360-758-2651), and the **Loganita** (360-758-2651).

The Gulf Islands

For the record, the Gulf Islands aren't in a gulf; they are in the Strait of Georgia, which forms the boundary between the U.S. and Canada. When the famed explorer Capt. George Vancouver cruised through the cluster of islands, he thought he was in a gulf and named it the Gulf of Georgia. The mistake is easy to forgive because when you're on a boat amid the islands, it is easy to believe you are surrounded by land. When later explorers found Vancouver's error, the waterway was renamed the Strait of Georgia.

Originally the entire group of islands was named in honor of Lopez de Haro, who discovered them in 1789. Then another Spanish explorer, Lt. Juan Francisco de Eliza, came through on June 24, 1791, the birthday of San Juan Bautista, viceroy of Mexico, and renamed the group in his honor. The whole archipelago remained under this Spanish umbrella until the English and Americans finally asked Germany's Kaiser Wilhelm to determine the international boundary. When this happened, the Americans kept the San Juan name, and the British, wanting their own nomenclature, chose to call their group the Gulf Islands. In this way, one might say, the politicians split up a happy family of islands.

The Gulf group numbers more than 250 pieces of land that qualify as islands. Like their American neighbors, the number includes several very large rocks that always remain above high tide. Eight islands—Pender, Saturna, Mayne, Galiano, Saltspring, Thetis, Kuper and Gabriola—have permanent populations. Saltspring is the largest with

7,500 residents. Pender Island(s) is next in population with about 1,500. The others are below 1,000.

Many of the smaller Gulf Islands have modest populations in spite—and in some cases because of—the lack of ferry service; the typical islander is an independent sort who wants to live away from cities, traffic and freight trains that whistle through the night. They move to remote areas to be left alone, so this book will honor that wish by sticking to islands that are served by public ferries in both countries.

B.C. ferries headed west from Tsawwassen call on Galiano, Mayne, Saturna, Pender and Saltspring, in that order. Saltspring is also served by a ferry from Crofton on Vancouver Island which docks at Vesuvius on the northern part of Saltspring. Farther north, two islands separate from the Gulf group, Thetis and Kuper islands, are served by a ferry from Chemainus. Gabriola, the farthest north of the group, is served by a ferry from Nanaimo.

Reservations are required for vehicles traveling from the mainland (Tsawwassen) to the Gulf Islands, but reservations are not required for vehicles from Vancouver Island (Swartz Bay) going to the islands. Nor are reservations required for inter-island travel. Walk-on passengers never need reservations. For ferry information: mainland, 604-669-1211; Victoria, 604-386-3431; Saltspring Island, 604-537-9921; other southern Gulf Islands, 604-629-3215.

If your visit is to be a short one, it is sometimes easier and cheaper to leave your car on the mainland and rely on public transportation once you arrive than it is to spend hours in ferry lines and then pay the ferry fare. Bus transportation is available at the terminals at Swartz Bay, 604-382-9921, and Tsawwassen (B.C. Transit), 604-521-0400. Or phone Pacific Coach, 604-662-7575.

The Gulf Islands aren't as crowded as the San Juans, and most residents hope they never become so. One reason for the low population and development density is a fundamental difference in approach to self-government. Much local control of the San Juans has been dominated by real estate interests, and several rousing battles have been fought between developers and preservationists.

Conversely, the Gulf Islands are subject to the dictates of the Island Trust, created in 1974 by the provincial government in Victoria to help preserve the islands' rural character and to control new development. The trust came into being as the result of a subdivision named Magic Lakes Estates which suddenly appeared on the southwest end of North Pender. The cluster of homes look like any other subdivision on the outskirts of any major North American city—crowded, small ordinary houses and too many for the water table and septic drainage fields to accommodate. It wasn't at all the kind of thing most people expected when they moved to the islands; it was one of the things they moved to the islands to avoid. They saw the subdivision as one version of the future being built before their eyes and didn't like it at all. They went to Victoria to do something about it.

The Island Trust was the result. Its governing body is composed of two representatives from each island and, like any local governing body, it is frequently embroiled in controversy as it tries to accomplish the impossible task of pleasing everyone. However, it has prevented development of epidemic proportions on the islands, as you will see when you visit them or go past aboard a ferry. The sight warms the chilled hearts of conservationists and gives developers heartburn.

The first ferry stop out of Tsawwassen is at **Galiano,** a long—16 miles (26 km)—island and the driest of the group because it is east of the higher Saltspring Island, which catches most of the moisture that escapes Vancouver Island's mountains. Most of Galiano is controlled by MacMillan Bloedel and used as a tree farm, which leaves only a portion of the land for habitation. Most of the approximately 800 residents live on the southern end a short distance from the ferry landing at Sturdies Bay.

Galiano is a good place to find seldom-used beaches where the beachcombing can be rewarding. **Montague Provincial Park,** a short distance from the ferry landing, fronts on a broad beach with calm and warm waters in the protection of Parker Island just offshore. The park has campsites, picnic tables and hiking trails.

Galiano has a single pub, the **Hummingbird Inn Pub,** at the island's main intersection where Sturdies Bay, Georgeson Bay and Porlier Pass Roads converge. A scattering of other places to eat, some open only seasonally, are found around the island so it is best to explore or call the information number below before making plans. The same suggestion applies to shopping.

The island has several places to stay. Two of the most popular are **Bodega Resort,** which has log cabins (604-539-2677) and **Woodstone Country Inn** (604-539-2022), which features fireplaces in most rooms and pastoral rather than marine scenery.

For information: Galiano Island Visitors Association, 604-539-2233.

Mayne Island has one of the most colorful histories of the island group, and an impressive collection of homes, both historical and modern. Some people refer to Mayne as the Islander's Island because it is lightly developed and retains its original rural character.

It has several beautiful and seldom-used beaches, including Bennett Bay and Campbell Bay. Relatively new is **Dinner Bay Park,** a former farm with a beach, picnic and camping areas. The island is popular with bicyclists because it has so little traffic.

Several inns and B&Bs are dotted around the island, among them the **Maynecliffe B&B** (604-539-2236); **Blue Vista Resort,** which has housekeeping cabins (604-539-2463), and **Fernhill Lodge,** with theme rooms and a popular restaurant (604-539-2544).

Saturna Island is the least populated of the islands served by ferries and has very few places to stay or eat. It has no public campgrounds or parks nor does it have a loop drive. This makes it a less than attractive destination for most day-trippers, but bicyclists, boaters and kayakers like it for its many coves and inlets with beaches bare of humanity. Hikers like to climb Mount Warburton Pike for the view and to see the feral goats that live in the area.

Saturna has a general store and one B&B, the **Stone House Farm Resort,** with three rooms and an oceanfront cottage (604-539-2683).

The proper name for **Pender Island** is plural, Penders, although very few pronounce it that way. Until just after the turn of this century, Pender was one island with an exaggerated hour-glass shape. The squeezed part formed a narrow isthmus which presumably had been two beaches on neighboring islands that gradually silted up over the centuries to create one island. Citizens who had to row around the island took a short cut by dragging their boats across this narrow neck. Over the years they got tired of this and talked the government into digging a channel for small boats, which was accomplished in 1903.

Then, after half a century having to row across the channel, they went back to the government and in 1955 got a bridge across the gap. Island historians like to point out that when this occurred, researchers could find no record that the government had approved digging the canal in the first place, even though it was government employees with government equipment who did so. In spite of this confusion, and speculation that something funny may have happened half a century earlier, the provincial government provided funds for the one-lane wooden bridge spanning the channel today.

The Boon to Canadian Distillers

During the late years of the 19th century, smugglers worked the Gulf and San Juan islands with their liquor, drugs, illegal immigrants and anything else that wasn't supposed to be shipped across the borders. The smuggling reached its apex during the United States' peak experience in legislated morality, better known as Prohibition, which banned the production and sale of alcoholic beverages in the country.

Rum runners in boats built for either speed or silence sneaked in and out of the islands, trying to evade the badly outnumbered American "Revenuers" whose job was like trying to dam the

The result of all this is North Pender and South Pender, or simply Penders, with a common post office. According to one source, a certain reserve exists between the North and the South Penderites, a throwback to 90 years ago when the walkers and the boaters argued over digging the channel. If the American Civil War is still being fought emotionally in the United States, why not the Pender Pique?

The Penders are next to Saltspring in population and popularity with visitors. They have some of the best weather in B.C., thanks to a microclimate called Mediterranean that gives them only 17 to 22 inches (43 to 55 cm) of rainfall each year.

The islands have at least fifteen beaches open to the public, and the waters in some are popular for swimming because they are protected and shallow. You can rent rowboats and sailboats to explore. Many visitors bring their canoes or kayaks to paddle in the more remote areas around the islands. Bicycles can be rented near the ferry landing at Otter Bay. Bike-route maps are provided.

You have several choices of parks with picnic areas and overnight campgrounds. **Prior Centennial Provincial Park** overlooking Browning Harbour and **Beaumont Provincial**

stream of booze with fish net. It is said that one of the favorite places for smugglers to hole up during the daylight hours was along the shore of South Pender Island because it has so many nooks and crannies. This truly dumb chapter in American history lasted from 1920 until 1933, and nobody was sadder to see it end than Canadian distillers and the smugglers who provided Americans with good Canadian whisky.

Americans are justified in saying, "You're welcome, Vancouver," when they look at the Lions Gate Bridge because it was a gift to the city from the Seagrams distilling family.

Marine Park are two of the most popular. The latter, on South Pender Island, is accessible only by boat or on foot.

The islands have two main shopping areas, at Hope Bay, where you'll find a general store and a government wharf, and Port Washington, which has a small shopping center. Many specialized shops are scattered throughout the islands, such as the general stores at Bedwell Harbour and Otter Bay.

You'll find several good places to eat in the towns—Bedwell Harbour, Otter Bay, Port Washington—and scattered along the roads and on the waterfront. Some popular places are **Campbell's Pender Bakery** and **Bob's Driftwood Café.** The **Whale Pod** at Bedwell Harbour Resort is unpretentious and friendly.

Lodging is no particular problem because of a growing B&B industry and a number of long-established inns and resorts. **Bedwell Harbour Resort** on South Pender (closed from October to April) is casual and popular (604-629-3212). **Cliffside Inn-on-the-Sea** on North Pender serves enormous breakfasts (604-629-6691). The **Pender Lodge,** also on the north island, is perhaps the largest; it has separate cottages in addition to rooms (604-629-3221).

The largest Gulf Island by far is **Saltspring;** it is more than three times as large as number-two Galiano, and its population of about 7,500 is 6,000 more than Pender Islands. It is so large that it has ferry service to each end: the Tsawwassen-to-Swartz Bay ferry lands at Long Harbour, the Swartz Bay-to-Tsawwassen ferry lands at Fulford, and another ferry runs from Crofton on Vancouver Island to Vesuvius Bay on Saltspring's northern end.

The island's size has spawned a joke that it gets to spell its name two ways, Saltspring and Salt Spring. Not all residents are amused by such comments. I still don't know which is correct. I read somewhere that it was always two words until a bureaucrat jammed them together on a legal document, and so they remained. The name refers to more than a dozen springs on the north end of the island, on private property, which produce brackish water that stains plant life white.

On maps and from airplanes, the island looks as if it were squeezed in two places, making it into three pieces linked together. It is mountainous on the south end, then the mountains give way to hills and gently rolling land on the north end, where most of the population is centered. Ganges, at the north end, is the island's main town, and subdivisions are spreading outward. Other small towns are Fulford Harbour, Fernwood and Vesuvius.

The island's terrain includes mountains, plains and several beaches, making it popular with outdoors people. You'll find several parks, both local and provincial. **Ruckle Provincial Park** is one of the most popular because it has a beach, is very level, and is only 6 miles (10 km) from the Fulford ferry landing. You will often see backpackers trudging off the ferry, bound for the park.

Mount Maxwell Provincial Park, as its name implies, is on high ground. Roughly in the middle of the island, the park isn't overly developed, but its loop trails lead to nice views of the island and strait. It also serves as a buffer for an ecological reserve established to protect a stand of Garry oak, the only oak native to British Columbia.

You can drive to Bruce Peak, 2,300 feet (698 m), the tallest point in the Gulf Islands, but you'll have to share the view with a microwave tower and a forestry lookout tower. The view includes the mainland of British Columbia and Washington, much of Vancouver Island and northward on the Inside Passage. You may also share the summit with hang gliders, who soar off the summit like fixed-wing butterflies, headed to landing spots near sea level.

For those who like their activities at sea level, or nearly so, the many lakes and saltwater bays and coves make the island popular for sailors, canoeists and kayakers. Several of the lakes are open to the public, and five or six of them are good for fishing. The island is also noted for its good scuba diving, which is covered in a separate chapter.

As you would expect on such a busy island, it has several good cafés and restaurants. Among them are the **Bouzouki Greek Café** with sea views (604-537-4181), and **The Inn at Vesuvius** near the dock at Vesuvius Bay (604-537-2312).

Following Pages:
The view from Hurricane
Ridge in Olympic National
Park—a sea of mountains
WASHINGTON STATE TRAVEL

If you are looking for gentility, the most popular place to stay on Saltspring is the **Hastings House,** near Ganges. You don't rent a room here—you rent a suite, and they come furnished with wood stoves, down quilts, thick carpets and expensive furniture. The house has perhaps the island's most upscale restaurant; breakfast is free for guests but the elaborate dinners are separate. For all of this you pay a great deal—in excess of $300 per night in the summer (604-537-2362).

Not all travelers require a hotel experience; some just want a clean, quiet and safe place to sleep. You can get a very nice place to stay for $50 or less at one of the motels around the island. Other good bets are the family resorts, such as **Booth Bay Resort** (604-537-5651). If you don't require saltwater views, **St. Mary Lake** has a cluster of rental cabins around it.

Information: Saltspring Island Infocentre, 604-537-5252.

THE OLYMPIC PENINSULA ROUTE

 Many travelers headed for Vancouver Island drive to Port Angeles so they can take the M/V *Coho* to downtown Victoria. This route usually involves a ride on a Washington State Ferry from Seattle to Bainbridge Island, which is connected to the Kitsap Peninsula—a finger of the Olympic Peninsula—by the Agate Pass Bridge on the west side of Bainbridge Island. Another major route is from Edmonds across to Kingston on the Kitsap Peninsula. The route crosses Hood Canal, which is not a canal but a fjord, on the Hood Canal Floating Bridge, one of the few such bridges in the world.

Just before you arrive at the bridge, you will drive through the tiny town of **Port Gamble,** a well-tended remnant of the pioneer years of logging. The town was built by Pope and Talbot, a lumber company out of Maine that bought several thousand acres on the peninsula and built a sawmill at the site of the town. The houses and public buildings, including a beautiful church, were patterned somewhat after the company's town of origin, East Machias, Maine. The entire town is still owned by Pope and Talbot, and homes are rented, at reasonable rates, to company employees. Port Gamble has a museum in the general store that is worth a visit.

Once you are across the bridge and on the main part of the Olympic Peninsula, you can drive straight to Port Angeles or take a side trip to Port Townsend. Most people who come to the area on vacation include Port Townsend because its homes and public buildings constitute one of the best examples of Victorian architecture north of Eureka, California.

At one time **Port Townsend** was the major city in Washington. It had several foreign consuls and the U.S. Customs station, and everyone in town was convinced it would become the dominant city in the fledgling state. However, these hopes were dashed when the transcontinental railroad stopped on the east side of Puget Sound, making Tacoma and then Seattle the dominant cities. Port Townsend went into a period of decline and benign neglect and didn't start rising again until the 1960s when so many successful entrepreneurs decided to chuck urban life for small towns. Port Townsend became the darling of Puget Sound and a favorite destination for day trips and weekends away from home.

It certainly has the raw material for an interesting destination town. In addition to the dozens of carpenter-gothic Victorian houses and public buildings, the Army built **Fort Worden** on the tip of the Quimper Peninsula. When it became obsolete, it was turned over to Washington State Parks, which made it into an artists' colony directed by the Centrum Foundation. Throughout the year Centrum holds workshops and conferences for writers, artists and musicians. Some of the highlights are the annual jazz festival, a writers conference, the Festival of American Fiddle Tunes, various classical music concerts and art events.

The park rents the former officers' row homes, but the waiting list is very long. However, Port Townsend has one of the largest concentrations of bed and breakfasts and inns in the region, most in historic homes. Its hotels range from a very ordinary motel along the main drag to the modest grandeur of rooms in the **Manresa Castle**. This imposing edifice on the hill south of town, dating back to 1892, was built to look like a French chateau by a wealthy man as a gift to his wife. It was later used as a monastery before being resurrected again as a good hotel.

Long after it became a hotel its bathrooms were still at each end of the long halls. It is a condition some people find endearing but Hollywood doesn't. When the movie *An Officer and a Gentleman* was filmed around town and Fort Worden, the movie crew's contracts stipulated that they stay in hotels with bathrooms in the rooms. Port Townsend didn't have enough rooms to house the crew, so the studio struck a deal with Manresa Castle: The film company paid the hotel some of the room rent up front on the condition that the hotel use the money to install bathrooms. It still doesn't have a bathroom for every room—some must share—but it is far better than having to join the parade of strangers down the hall in your robe.

Through the good fortune of having the Centrum Foundation at Fort Worden State Park, with its concerts and conferences, Port Townsend sponsors a series of events that draw people from all over the region. The town also is home to the Wooden Boat Foundation, which holds several gatherings of boat builders and collectors each year.

Information: Port Townsend Chamber of Commerce, 2437 Sims Way, Port Townsend, 98368. Phone: 360-385-2722.

The 50-mile (80-km) drive from Port Townsend to Port Angeles runs along a pretty stretch of Highway 101 with frequent views of saltwater and the Olympic Mountains. The largest town between the two "port" cities is **Sequim** (pronounced Skwim), which is famous for being in the driest zone on the Olympic Peninsula. This "rain shadow effect" or "blue hole" is caused by the mountains catching the clouds blown in by the prevailing southwest wind. The tallest mountains catch most of the moisture so Sequim gets only about 17 inches (43 cm) of rain per year whereas all around the dry strip the rainfall is double, treble or even quadruple that amount. Sequim is a popular retirement area, so be prepared for very slow drivers as you go through town.

Port Angeles is more or less the focal point of the Olympic Peninsula. The Olympic National Park's headquarters are there, it is the major shipping port for the region, and the point of departure for Victoria.

When you arrive, drive down toward the ferry dock and park on the waterfront at the Municipal Pier and Marine Laboratory. You will be less than a block from the ferry terminal and the town's information center. Nearby is the **Arthur D. Feiro Marine Laboratory,** operated by the local community college, with hands-on exhibits. Admission. Information: 360-452-9277.

If you're taking your vehicle to Vancouver Island, the early morning departure may force you to stay overnight in Port Angeles. It is a good idea to spend at least two days in the area so you can visit **Olympic National Park,** recently declared a World Heritage Park.

This is one of Washington's prime destinations, and one of the most beautiful parks in the American system. It covers more than 900,000 acres (365 000 ha) and has virtually no roads through it. You can walk through these silent, moss-covered forests on trails along the Hoh and Soleduck rivers, but be prepared for rain. They are called rain forests for a very good reason: annual rainfall reaches 140 inches (355 cm).

The main part of the park encompasses the heart of the Olympic Mountains and the valleys created by rivers flowing down from the snow and glaciers to the ocean. One must-see spot is the heavily visited **Hurricane Ridge** 17 miles (27 km) south of Port Angeles in the heart of the mountains. The drive to the mile-high ridge takes you first through thick forest that gradually thins out until you go above timberline. The road winds around open ridges until it at last stops at the Hurricane Ridge Lodge. Here you will almost feel as if you're hang gliding over the mountains and valleys. The lodge is a combination visitor center, café, gift shop and interpretive center.

Back down almost to sea level is **Lake Crescent,** my favorite lake in the state. Although Highway 101 runs along its southern shore, Lake Crescent is large enough to make the traffic and attendant noise seem insignificant.

The lake is surrounded by dramatic mountains and its shores are dotted with picturesque trees and boulders. Three large lodges are operated by National Park concessions. **Lake Crescent Lodge** has a main lodge and cottages that were built for the visit of President Franklin D. Roosevelt in 1937. **Log Cabin Resort,** on the northeast end of the lake, is similar to Lake Crescent Lodge, but not as elaborate. Trails ranging in length from leg-stretchers to day hikes lead off the shore. The interior of the park has numerous trails for more serious backpacking.

A major function of Port Angeles is to serve as a jumping off place for Canada's Vancouver Island. The 1,000-passenger M.V. *Coho,* owned by Black Ball Transport, makes the 1-1/2-hour run four times a day during the busy summer months and drops back to twice a day during the winter. The ferry also hauls vehicles ranging from bicycles to 18-wheelers. Be aware that during the summer the wait to board a vehicle can stretch to five or six hours as the line inches along at each sailing. Thus, if you plan to visit only Victoria you can park your car near the *Coho* terminal for around $5 a day and go as a foot passenger. The ferry is often quite crowded but has an adequate number of places to sit, both inside and outside. Cafeteria. Information: 360-457-4491.

You also have the option of taking the *Victoria Express,* a faster, passenger-only boat that makes up to four crossings daily netween Port Angeles and Victoria during the summer. The trip takes about an hour each way and costs roughly half the *Coho* fare. Information: 206-622-2222 or 206-452-8088.

Vancouver's high-rise landscape >
contrasts with Stanley Park's
forested acres; beyond lie
English Bay and the North
Shore and Coast Mountains.
Tourism Vancouver

Vancouver

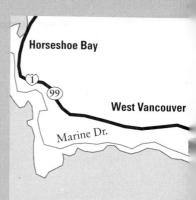

Horseshoe Bay

West Vancouver

Marine Dr.

Burrard Inlet

Spanish Banks

5

W. 16th Ave.

S.W. Marine Dr.

Sea
Island

N

While all three cities of the Evergreen Triangle rank high on lists of the world's most beautiful cities, Vancouver has been fortunate in its selection of city planners with a continuing concern for the quality of life for the city's residents. More than most large cities, Vancouver remains on a human scale and meets one major criterion for greatness: it is a pleasant city for walking.

This most picturesque of cities is surrounded on three sides by saltwater. Its downtown sits on gently hilly land that, across Burrard Inlet, suddenly soars upward to become steep, dramatic mountains. Burrard Inlet, which surrounds the Vancouver peninsula, is a long fjord which runs several miles inland before splitting into two arms. Indian Arm swings north into the mountains while the Inlet continues a short distance before ending at the community of Port Moody.

The heart of Vancouver is a hooked peninsula surrounded by English Bay on the west, False Creek on the south, Burrard Inlet on the north and Coal Harbour on the northeast. Almost half of the Vancouver peninsula is given over to Stanley Park, one of the largest and most beautiful urban parks in North America. Most of Vancouver's residential and small business neighborhoods, and its downtown core, are situated south of Burrard Inlet. Among the most desirable places to live are the north shore communities of North Vancouver and West Vancouver. Both communities are joined to Vancouver proper by two bridges, Lions Gate, reached by a causeway through Stanley Park, and the Second Narrows Bridge, which crosses Burrard Inlet farther east.

A still larger peninsula is formed by the Fraser River which runs down to sea from Central British Columbia and flows almost parallel to Burrard Inlet south of Vancouver before entering the Strait of Georgia. Where the river forks to form Lulu Island, the north bank of this arm becomes the southern city limits of Vancouver.

Vancouver has little choice but to spread south and east because it is jammed up against steep mountains all along its northern edge. This constriction has forced development south toward the U.S. border in the growing towns of Richmond and White Rock, and east along the Fraser River Valley.

Many Americans are surprised that a city as large as Vancouver and with as much traffic does not have a freeway running through its heart. The basic fact is that the citizenry does not want one. Another answer is a question: Where would it go? Unlike Victoria and Seattle, Vancouver isn't really on the way to somewhere else. Nearly all of the south-to-north traffic and all of the east-to-west routes stop in the city. Obviously some continues north to the recreation area of Whistler and beyond, and some goes to the ferries at the Horseshoe Bay landing northwest of town, but not enough to justify tearing up the city and building new bridges across Burrard Inlet. Thus, most of Vancouver's traffic is on two- and four-lane streets with traffic signals. Nevertheless, traffic moves smoothly, even during rush hour, mostly because basic courtesy is practiced on the streets; you will seldom see a clogged intersection.

Visiting motorists should be aware that few streets have left-turn lanes; on four-lane streets the inside lanes are often the slowest because of drivers waiting to make left turns. Most traffic clings to the outside lane, which is also the lane used by transit busses, which stop frequently. You'll quickly learn to join locals in darting back and forth between the lanes like demented waterbugs.

Vancouver is easily the most cosmopolitan of the three cities with its lively mix of nationalities. Its cultural diversity includes Chinatown, where you will hear Mandarin or Cantonese spoken almost everywhere. People of Chinese origin form the second largest ethnic group in British Columbia, after the British. There are also sizable contingents of German, French, Dutch, Scandinavian, Ukrainian and Italian ancestry, many of whom are first-generation immigrants.

Unlike the United States, newcomers to Canada aren't urged to assimilate and leave the culture of their homeland behind. About a quarter of British Columbians are first-generation immigrants. Ethnic groups tend to settle in "pockets" of the city. Vancouver also has its "Little Italy" and its significant East Indian community. Each community has given rise to its own specialty stores and restaurants, so it's as easy to find "boerkoel" (kale, a leafy vegetable eaten by the Dutch) in Vancouver as it is to find it in Amsterdam.

The Dutch have made an impact on agriculture in the outlying areas of Vancouver where they own dairy farms and flower bulb fields. Germans form the third largest ethnic group in British Columbia. Their ancestors were originally drawn to Canada by the British Columbia Gold Rush of the 1800s. While most did not make their fortunes in gold, they stayed to earn a comfortable living as grocers, farmers, craftsmen, shopkeepers and brewers.

Native Indians, who prefer to be known as First Nations people, form a significant portion of British Columbia society, and awareness of the significance of West Coast native culture is increasing. The character of most West Coast art, and even architecture, borrows bits and pieces from the art of the Haida, Kwakiutl and Nuu-Chah-Nulth tribes of the coastal regions. (The Nuu-Chah-Nulth people recently changed their tribal name from Nootka, a misinterpretation of the name by English-speaking people.) In recent years, totem-pole carving has undergone a renaissance, and native art from British Columbia turns up in collections around the world.

This rich cultural and ethnic mix keeps Vancouver from becoming a homogenized city with only a few distinctive "looks." You can drive though neighborhoods and find enclaves of Tudor architecture just down the street from neighborhoods of recent immigrants from Hong Kong who build new homes or remodel old ones to suit their cultural needs. In shopping districts you can find food, clothing, furnishings and gifts from virtually every country in the world and hear the languages and see the style of dress from those countries. It is doubtful that any city in the world has a greater cultural, racial, religious and social mix than Vancouver.

Although one would expect all this diversity to create a lot of friction, Canadians seem to be more tolerant than Americans and while racial tensions obviously exist, the social system encourages courteous behaviour.

In business circles, Vancouverites are as aggressive as

their counterparts anywhere. One proof: the city's success as the second largest port on the North American west coast (only Long Beach, California, is larger) and its enormously profitable Canada Place cruise-ship terminal, which is home port to nearly every ship on the busy Inside Passage route.

PUBLIC TRANSPORTATION

Vancouver provides an excellent interconnected public transportation which includes bus, rail and boat routes. B.C. Transit operates three major systems: city busses; the SeaBus between North Vancouver and downtown Vancouver; and the SkyTrain. You can transfer from any of these three modes of travel to any other for the same fare.

The Blue Bus system (604-985-7777) is an extension of West Vancouver's system which links Vancouver and the B.C. Ferries terminal at Horseshoe Bay. These busses

SkyTrain Outings

If you want to get out of the city for a day, you can take a nice outing on the SkyTrain to the New Westminister stop at Westminister Quay where you'll find a public market similar to that in Vancouver. The quay overlooks the Fraser River, and beautifully maintained tugboats are tied up by the shopping center. Also at the quay, a tugboat replica named "Tugger" was built for children to play on, and you can go aboard the Samson V, a historic paddlewheeler that is now a museum.

For another shorter outing, take the SeaBus to its North Vancouver terminus at the Lonsdale Quay. The shopping center on the quay is one of those aromatic, eclectic public markets where you can buy flowers, chocolate, wine, fresh fish, fruits and vegetables and various treats.

depart from Homer and Georgia streets beside the post office and run along West Georgia Street and across the Lions Gate Bridge.

The SeaBus system consists of two 400-passenger high-speed catamarans, the *Burrard Otter* and the *Burrard Beaver,* which make frequent crossings (every 13 minutes during the day, every 30 mintues at night) between a dock at the foot of Granville Street, adjacent to Canada Place, and Lonsdale Quay at the foot of Lonsdale Boulevard in North Vancouver. Passengers are funneled to and from the dock through the handsome, renovated CPR station. The SeaBus is at least a partial answer to the traffic congestion caused by the narrow Lions Gate Bridge, and it has been very successful.

The SkyTrain is an automated rapid-transit system that runs from the same waterfront station at Canada Place to the suburban cities of New Westminister and Surrey. Trains arrive and depart every three to five minutes during the day and make 17 stops between its terminals in downtown Vancouver and Surrey. Information: 604-521-0400.

Two passenger railroads operate out of Vancouver. The national system, VIA Rail, offers thrice-weekly departures eastward across the Rockies to Eastern Canada from the former Canadian National Railway station at Main and Station streets (see below). VIA information: 604-669-3050 or 1-800-561-8630 (in Canada), 1-800-561-3949 (in U.S.). B.C. Rail operates one passenger train a day out of North Vancouver which goes north to Lillooet daily and to Prince George three times a week via Squamish, Whistler and Lillooet. It departs from the station at 1311 W. First St., North Vancouver (604-631-3500). A city bus leaves the VIA Rail station and connects with this early morning train, and also meets the returning evening train to take passengers back to Vancouver.

The most visible air service in Vancouver is Air B.C., a connector line for Air Canada that flies turboprop float planes from Coal Harbour on an hourly schedule to Victoria's Inner Harbour. The trip takes 25 minutes. Information: 604-688-5515 (Vancouver), 604-360-9074 (Victoria) or 1-800-730-7171 (U.S.). Canadian Regional

Airlines, which is Canadian Airlines' connector, makes similar flights between Vancouver International Airport and Victoria International Airport, using similar planes on the 20-minute flight. Information: 604-279-6611. In Victoria, call 382-6111; from the U.S., 1-800-426-7000.

The latest news in Vancouver transportation is the 1993 transformation of the old Canadian National Station into the Pacific Central Station. The station is home to VIA Rail and the tour train Rocky Mountaineer, plus Greyhound, Maverick and Pacific Coach Lines busses. It is also adjacent to the Main Street stop for SkyTrain.

SIGHTSEEING

Parks and Gardens

Stanley Park. This magnificent park covers 1,000 acres (400 ha) of beautiful virgin forest, broad and green lawns, lakes and ponds, and numerous places to sit and stare or walk or jog. It is considerably larger than New York City's 840-acre (340-ha) Central Park, and much, much safer. A road and a paved trail circles the park. A complete circuit of 6.5 miles (10.5 km) gives you sea level views of Burrard Inlet, the Strait of Georgia and English Bay. Numerous trails wind through the park. The Vancouver Aquarium, a miniature train, a petting zoo and a large collection of totem poles are located on its eastern side. In the summer, special "Around the Park" busses function for non-perambulators.

Cypress Provincial Park. This park above West Vancouver has some of the most spectacular views of the whole city and beyond. One of the best viewpoints is only a short distance from where the road leaves the main highway. You reach the park by driving west toward Horseshoe Bay on Highway 1, exiting at the Cypress Park turnoff and following the twisting 5-mile (8-km) road to the summit. You don't have to go all the way to the top for good hiking trails, but the most spectacular ones are up there. Nordic skiers love the mountain's more than 16 miles (26 km) of interconnected and groomed trails on Hollyburn Ridge. Its 25 downhill runs are equally popular and at 1,750 feet (533 m) it has the longest vertical drop of any of the North Shore ski areas.

Grouse Mountain. 6400 Nancy Greene Way, North Vancouver (604-984-0661). Any time you are in Vancouver on a perfectly clear day (they are getting more and more rare), treat yourself to one of the most spectacular views in the world by driving up winding Capilano Road in North Vancouver to 3,600-foot (1100-m) Grouse Mountain. This is the mountain with the lights you see from downtown; and especially on winter evenings, when it is being used for night skiing, probably a few rear-end automobile accidents have been caused by people gawking at the spectacle of lights seeming to float in the air.

Take the 50-passenger tram up the mountain for an unforgettable panorama over almost the entire city: English Bay, Washington State's Mount Baker, the Strait of Georgia and parts of Vancouver Island. During the winter a modest ski run operates there. You can eat in the Grouse Nest restaurant and Jumpers Bistro, and you'll never have a better view with a meal. The Theater in the Sky has a multimedia show in a 140-seat theater. The mountain is also

Pacific Coast Totems

They stand silent and stately on promontories and in parks overlooking broad expanses of sheltered waterways where war canoes once cruised. Some have been relocated to museums, looking caged and fierce like the wild creatures they depict. Wherever totems are found today they serve as a reminder of a time when Native American tribes dominated the coastline of the Inside Passage from Puget Sound to Alaska.

Time is taking its toll on the original poles and only a few remain in situ. Most of what you will see today have been gathered into major collections for protection against the elements. The best museum collections in the Ever-

very popular with hang gliders; world championships are held there frequently. Helicopter tours are available from the mountain for those who don't want to fly alone.

Mount Seymour Provincial Park. Skiing information: 604-986-2261. This park is one of the most popular year-round destinations for Vancouverites. During non-skiing months it is used by hikers, mountain bikers, backpackers and picnickers. In winter its four double chairlifts and one rope tow go into business. An extensive network of snowshoeing and cross-country skiing trails wind through the park. It has a day lodge and a cafeteria. Snowboarding is also popular and boards can be rented on the mountain, as can snowshoes and cross-country skis.

Pacific Spirit Park. Information: 604-224-5739. One of the newest parks in the Vancouver area also has the distinction of being the largest urban park in North America. This 2,500-acre (1000-ha) park is part of the University of British Columbia's endowment lands that were given to the university to sell off as needed. The university kept the land, a small portion of which is virgin timber. Pacific Spirit

green Triangle are in Vancouver and Victoria. Perhaps the most dramatic collection of all is in the University of British Columbia's Museum of Anthropology. Other excellent collections are in Stanley Park and in the Capilano Suspension Bridge and Regional Park in North Vancouver.

Understanding totems is a major anthropological undertaking, and although certain symbols—the mythical thunderbird, the whale, eagle, raven, beaver, bear—are found in most poles, the meaning varies from pole to pole and band, tribe or family.

The possession of a totem pole was the lifelong ambition of every Northwest Coast Native, and much of his power within the clan or tribe came from the size and ➤

Park forms the eastern boundary of the university campus and it stretches from the north arm of the Fraser River to English Bay. Its 33 miles (58 km) of hiking trails are sparsely used. At the information center on 16th Avenue you can get trail guides and sign up for walks with naturalists. Free.

Queen Elizabeth Park and Bloedel Floral Conservatory. 33rd and Cambie streets. Park and Conservatory, 604-872-5513; Seasons in the Park Restaurant, 874-8008. Queen E Park, as locals call it, was built on Little Mountain, at 492 feet (150 m) the highest point in Vancouver. The city took over two old quarries and built sunken gardens in them, along with numerous waterfalls, paths and a magnificent display of plants, creating Canada's first civic arboretum. The Bloedel Floral Conservatory, a 140-foot (42-m) plexiglass dome, protects more than 500 species and varieties of plants from jungles to deserts. Included in the park are tennis courts, a pitch and putt golf course, bowling greens and a restaurant. Admission to Conservatory.

Capilano Suspension Bridge and Park. 3735 Capilano Road, North Vancouver (604-985-7474). One of Vancouver's oldest attractions, this 5-foot (1.5-m) wide swinging

design of this status symbol. Totems were also judged by the status of the carver commissioned to do the carving. Thus carvers, who were as respected then as now, were some of the most wealthy people of the time.

When and how the carving began has been lost in oral history, and it probably would not have developed at all without cedar, the primary material for totems. Cedar is soft, straight-grained, has natural oils that protect it from rot for decades, and it ages to a wonderful silver-gray when it is not decorated with paints and stains.

The poles served several functions. Some were simply to welcome guests. Others were house poles with the house entrance cut into the base of the pole. Some were mortuary foot bridge hangs suspended 230 feet (70 m) above the Capilano Canyon. It was built in 1889 and has been one of the most popular attractions in the area.

Costumed staff members lead groups across from May to September. The complex includes a restaurant, nature park and gift shop. Anthropology and forestry tours are also conducted around the area. A native carver works on site all year long.

West Vancouver Centennial Seawalk. This 1-mile (1.6-km) walk is one of those places that locals are wont to label "typically Vancouverish" or some such description. It is a paved promenade along the seawall that parallels Marine Drive in West Vancouver's Ambleside, and is equally as popular as the seawall of Stanley Park. The main thing that sets this one apart is that dogs are not allowed on the pathway. They are, however, permitted to walk behind a fence, so every day dozens of dogs and owners are seen strolling briskly along the promenade, humans on the seaward side, dogs on the other side of the fence. The level, paved walk begins at John Lawson Park at 17th Street and leads westward to just beyond 30th Street.

poles, placed either at the grave like a headstone or designed to hold the ashes in a box on top. Still others were used inside as decorated house posts.

While it was common to add wings and bills to complete the visages, most relied on figures being carved out of the original tree trunk, and it was in this challenging carving that the best artists flourished, their imaginations soaring within the confined quarters.

Carvers are still honored among the Tlingits, the Haidas, Kwakiutls, Salish and Nuu-Chah-Nulths. Indeed, few Pacific Northwest Coast native people achieve more honor among their fellow tribesmen. As always, the best carvers have years of commissions awaiting.

Van Dusen Botanical Gardens. 5251 Oak Street (604-266-7194; Sprinklers Restaurant, 261-0011). This large botanical garden is an island of tranquility just off one of the city's busiest thoroughfares. The garden began as a golf course but grew into a major collection of ornamental plants from all over the world. It features pieces of sculpture placed strategically throughout the park, and the landscaping was designed around them after sculptors from all over the world were invited to work in local stone. The garden is divided into numerous areas, each representing a different geographic region of the world. A large collection of Asian plants is in the Sino-Himalayan Garden. Another popular area is the hedge maze for children. During December the garden is open every evening for its Festival of Lights with millions of Christmas lights strung throughout. It also has a gift shop. Admission.

Nitobe Memorial Garden. West Mall, University of British Columbia Campus (604-822-6038). This is a 2.5-acre (1-ha) Japanese garden with teahouse. It has authentic rock and sand gardens, Japanese plants and arched bridges across ponds. It is especially popular in the spring when cherry trees bloom, and in the autumn when maples and other trees turn colors.

Dr. Sun Yat-Sen Classical Chinese Garden. 578 Carroll St. (604-689-7133). This walled garden is the first authentic classical garden built outside China. It is typical of the Ming Dynasty period (1368-1644) in the Suzhou area. The garden buildings are handmade, from the roof tiles to the carved woodwork. Artisans came from China to Vancouver in 1985 and spent 13 months building the $5 million project. They brought everything needed to complete the garden, including the pebbles. Visitors will find a tranquility here that contrasts with the hustle and bustle just outside the gate. Admission.

This picturesque scene in >
Stanley Park is only a few blocks
away from Vancouver's
downtown core.
Tourism Vancouver

Guided Tours

Webfoot Walking Tours. Two women who love Vancouver's history and culture founded this tour company. Their tours cover Chinatown and, separately, downtown Vancouver. The Chinatown tour includes a look at the Sam Kee Building, which made the Guinness Book of Records as the world's narrowest building, a tea ceremony and a visit to a Taoist temple. The city tour includes Gastown, Robson Square, the Vancouver Art Gallery, Christ Church Cathedral and the Marine Building. Phone: 604-984-0842.

Gray Line of Vancouver. 200 - 399 W. 6th Ave. (604-879-3363). One of the largest guided-tour companies in Vancouver, Gray Line offers dinner cruises on tour boats with traditional salmon dinners and city tours in a doubledecker bus. Guides can conduct tours in five languages.

AAA Horse & Carriage. P.O. Box 1134, Station A (604-681-5115). This company operating at Grouse Mountain offers a variety of rides, by reservation, in horse-drawn carriages, including a 50-minute wagon ride in the summer and a 15-minute winter sleigh ride. The company also offers Stanley Park rides, leaving from the lower zoo parking lot.

Vancouver Trolley Company. 4012 Myrtle St., Burnaby (604-451-5581). This company runs two-hour loop trips during the summer months aboard antique streetcars showing the major attractions.

Special Places and Excursions

Gastown. This historic district, in the vicinity of Water, Carrall, Cordova and Powell streets, was one of the Evergreen Triangle pioneers in restored areas. Much of Vancouver's pioneer history occurred in Gastown. The area began as a sawmill. Then, in 1867, "Gassy Jack" Deighton came to the town that was called Hastings, opened his tavern, and his loquaciousness gave the district the nickname of Gastown. Three years later it was renamed Granville and 16 years later incorporated as the City of Vancouver. Like so many pioneer towns, Gastown was made almost entirely of wood and was levelled by fire in 1886. It came back as a commercial area and now is one of Vancouver's most trendy districts with warehouses converted to boutiques and restaurants. The center of Gastown is an old steam-powered clock at the corner of Cambie and Water.

Chinatown. This is the largest Chinese community in Canada. While Victoria's Chinatown is older—it dates back to 1858—the Vancouver community has grown more rapidly and has experienced a spurt of growth in recent years as many Hong Kong residents move to Canada. The first Chinese immigrants were brought to Canada in the late 1800s to work as laborers building the Canadian

< *The steam-powered clock—
a famous landmark in
Vancouver's Gastown district.*
TOURISM VANCOUVER

Pacific Railway, Canada's first transcontinental railway. Many came intending to become wealthy, then return to their families in China. However, low wages kept them in Canada, and when the railway was finished, they headed for the cities to congregate around their developing Chinatowns. Both areas have now been declared historic sites, assuring that their character will be preserved and enhanced.

Vancouver's Chinatown is gradually expanding, but its general boundaries are Gore on the east, East Georgia and Keefer on the south and East Pender on the north. The most significant Chinese architecture can be found along Pender. The Chinese Cultural Centre, 50 East Pender, sponsors

∧ *Typical store fronts in*
Vancover's busy Chinatown.

classes in arts and crafts and culture taught in both Chinese and English. It is connected to the Dr. Sun Yat-Sen Garden, described on page 116.

East Pender is the main street in Chinatown and in its crowded shops you will find Oriental herbal remedies, finely lacquered pots, jade jewelry, carved wood and handsome embroidered dresses and clothing. Many shops are filled with wonderful aromas.

The area is a wonderful place for strolling. You will see pharmacies which perform many of the functions normally associated with doctors. Large aquariums teem with food fish; barbecued chickens hang in windows; grocery stores have barrels and bins full of foods exotic to Western tastes. You will find all kinds of herbal products such as dried seahorses, dried snakes and lizards, black seaweed and jinseng; herbs that will prevent or cure seasickness, and herbs that will protect you from the common cold.

Some herbalists in Vancouver have built international reputations, and people of all races and cultures come to them for medical advice. Most work on a first-come, first-served basis. Inquire locally.

If you visit Vancouver without walking through Chinatown you will miss one of the city's richest experiences.

Vancouver Public Aquarium. Stanley Park (604-682-1118). More than 9,000 aquatic creatures are housed in the aquarium, including residents from the Arctic, the Amazon, Indonesia, and the Pacific Northwest. Perhaps its most popular mammals are the killer whales from Pacific Northwest and the white beluga whales from Arctic waters. The aquarium emphasizes, though, that these sea mammals are not trained to perform. Other residents include seals, sea otters, halibut, and several land creatures from the tropics, including boa constrictors, birds, bugs, poisonous frogs and turtles. Admission.

Science World. 1455 Quebec St. (604-268-6363). Housed in the domed Omnimax Theatre that was built for EXPO 86, Science World houses dozens of hands-on exhibits designed for youngsters, and the young at heart, who can learn about ocean waves, cosmic rays and lasers. The main gallery explains physics: You can light up a plasma ball or try to blow square bubbles. A "mazes" exhibit consists of a giant maze you can walk through. In the music gallery, you make music with your feet on a walk-on synthesizer. It also has a robotic cyclist and hot-air balloons. Other exhibits focus on the human body, earth sciences and leading-edge technology. Admission.

Granville Island. Beneath Granville Bridge. Information Centre: 1592 Johnston St. (604-666-5784). This peninsula on the south side of False Creek was an immediate hit with people from all over the Evergreen Triangle when, in 1972, it was transformed from a rundown industrial area into a completely new community. Many of the old factory sheds were remodeled and new buildings designed to fit into the industrial scheme. Corrugated roofing is prevalent, as is stucco siding and false fronts. Canopies have been color-coded so that red is for retail shops and green for recreation. The lively public market draws crowds daily, year-round. Artists have established studios; schools train new artists, and galleries show their works. Several theater groups rent space on the island and the Net Loft has several gift shops.

The island continues to change and develop, but its character is well established. Its cavernous buildings house more than 250 tenants; some have been set aside for theme shopping, including maritime shops and one called Kids Only. Numerous street performers—called buskers—earn extra money entertaining the thousands of visitors who visit daily.

You can drive onto the island, but the three-hour free parking spaces are usually difficult to find, so you may want to take public transportation, a taxi or ride a small ferry. Two companies operate these colorful ferries. Aquabus (604-689-5858) runs in summer between the Waterfront Theatre on Granville Island and the foot of Hornby Street. The Granville Island Ferry (604-684-7781) route includes the Bridges restaurant on the island, the Aquatic Centre at the northern end of Burrard Bridge, the Maritime Museum in Vanier Park, and Stamps Landing, a shopping area east of the island on False Creek.

B.C. Rail. 1311 West First Street, North Vancouver (604-984-5246). One of the best excursions out of Vancouver is the stretch of highway north along Howe Sound from Horseshoe Bay to Squamish, and one of the best ways to enjoy it is aboard B.C. Rail's unpretentious trains that chug along the narrow shelf between the mountains and the sound enroute to Lillooet and beyond.

As in all good voyages, the traveling is most of the fun because the train rocks along quietly and the scenery is never dull, even on an overcast or rainy day when the clouds come down to the surface of Howe Sound.

The railroad uses Budd trains, named for the manufacturer. More formally, they are known as RDCs, rail diesel cars. This species has no locomotive; the engineer sits at the front of the self-propelled car powered by twin 300-horse-

power engines. Sometimes the train crew invites passengers up to chat with the engineer.

The crews are a friendly group and not above playing practical jokes on the passengers. Often the conductor will alert the passengers that they can expect to see goats at a certain town along the way, implying that they will see mountain goats. But when the train slows for the flag-stop, he points to three domestic goats staked out beside the tracks. "I told you we'd see goats here, didn't I?" he asks brightly to a chorus of groans.

The regular B.C. Rail day trip goes to the historic town of Lillooet, with a two-hour layover before catching the afternoon train back to North Vancouver, giving passengers plenty of time to have lunch and to take a stroll through town. Or you can leave the train at Whistler/Blackcomb and spend the day at this international resort town. A shuttle bus meets the train's mid-morning arrival, but you will have to take a taxi to the station for the late afternoon return.

The railroad's printed schedule includes a mile-by-mile guide to the route which gives some of the more interesting historical information. It tells how Brandywine Falls came to be named: Members of a survey party were betting on its height, and one group bet wine against the other's brandy. Farther on, a tiny shack has a sign on it proclaiming it as 10

∧ *The Royal Hudson steam train skirts Howe Sound on its daily summer run between North Vancouver and Squamish.* Tourism Vancouver

North Downing. It was owned by a patriotic Englishman, and for years his dog met the train to collect its master's newspaper from the conductor. The station has another name, Gramson's, which makes it one of the few railroad stations in the world to have two names. British tourists love this station, and if the train isn't too far off schedule, the engineer will stop for passengers to take pictures of each other at the shack.

During the summer months the modest Budd cars are supplemented by the Royal Hudson, a historic steam-powered train that makes a daily round-trip run to Squamish. The beautifully restored coaches are very comfortable and the ride is a favorite with steam buffs. Nearly every morning you'll see photographers at vantage points along the track, recording this bit of history.

The Royal Hudson can be combined with a boat trip on the M.V. *Britannia,* one of Canada's largest excursion vessels. You catch the Royal Hudson from B.C. Railway's North Vancouver depot and ride it to Squamish, spend an hour in the small town, then return on the *Britannia.* The season goes from early June to mid-September. Advance booking is advised for individuals and required for groups of 20 or more.

CULTURE

Galleries

Vancouver has one of the liveliest art communities in Canada. New galleries and specialty museums continue to open each year. In early 1993, there were 71 operating galleries. About a dozen are clustered on Granville Island: the Textile Context Studio, Paperworks, Gallery of B.C. Ceramics, Creekhouse, and others. Another enclave has clustered on South Granville Street between West 15th Avenue and West 6th Avenue. Yet another is west of the Cambie Street Bridge on Cambie Street, and others are scattered through the downtown area and in Gastown.

Art Works, 225 Smithe St. (604-688-3301), handles pottery, fabrics, etched glass as well as paintings and graphics.

Bau-Xi, 3045 Granville St. (604-733-7011), has been a major factor in the promotion of contemporary Canadian art since 1966.

Bushlen/Mowatt Fine Arts, 1445 West Georgia St. (604-682-1234), handles international contemporary artists, mostly European.

Catriona Jefferies Gallery, 3149 Granville St. (604-736-1554), represents contemporary Canadian artists who are exploring post-modernist ideas.

Charles H. Scott Gallery, 1399 Johnston St. (604-844-3809), is in the Emily Carr College of Art and Design complex. It exhibits contemporary art and design.

Diane Farris Gallery, 1565 West 7th Ave. (604-737-2629), represents several contemporary Canadian artists.

Dorian Rae Collection, 3151 Granville St. (604-732-6100), specializes in collections of buddhas, tribal statues, masks and beads from Asia and Africa.

Equinox Gallery, 2321 Granville St. (604-736-2405), exhibits contemporary art from both Canada and the U.S., including painting, sculpture, photography and prints.

Federation Gallery, 1241 Cartwright St. (604-681-8534), is a federation of Canadian artists founded in 1941, and here some of British Columbia's best known artists exhibit their work.

Gallery of Tribal Art, 2329 Granville St. (604-732-4555), has artwork from Haida and other Northwest Coast people, New Guinea, Canadian and American Plains tribes.

Images For a Canadian Heritage, 164 Water St. (604-685-7046), specializes in Inuit and Northwest Coast artwork.

Malaspina Printmakers Gallery, 1555 Duranleau St. (604-688-1827), is a printmakers' cooperative that shows prints of members and associates.

Marion Scott Gallery, 801 West Georgia St. and 671 Howe St. (604-685-1934), handles contemporary British Columbia sculpture, Inuit and Northwest Coast native art.

Pentley Jones Gallery, 2245 Granville St. (604-732-5353), has drawings, paintings, watercolors and sculpture by British and Canadian artists.

Uno Langmann Fine Arts, 2117 Granville St. (604-736-8825), sells Old Master paintings from the 19th and early 20th centuries, and European and American antiques.

Museums

Museum of Anthropology. 6393 N.W. Marine Dr., University of British Columbia (604-822-3825). One of Vancouver's showcases, this world-class museum houses an enormous collection of art by First Nations people of the Pacific Northwest Coast. The building itself was inspired by native cedar longhouses and has won several awards for its architect, Arthur Erickson.

The museum's Great Hall contains one of the world's major collections of totems. Here you will find poles with ravens, bears, salmon, frogs and various human forms. Glass has been used extensively on the rear wall of the Great Hall to extend the indoor art outward. More weathered totem poles and Haida houses stand on the promontory known as Point Grey.

The museum commissioned several carvers to do pieces for its collection. Perhaps the best known is one by master carver Bill Reid called The Raven and the First Men. It shows a raven crouched on a clamshell filled with tiny human figures struggling to get out.

Several other collections unrelated to native culture include one of European ceramics. The museum hosts traveling exhibits and several special events throughout the year. It has a large museum shop. Admission.

Vancouver Art Gallery. 750 Hornby St. in Robson Square (604-682-5621). The name of this fine institution confuses some Americans, who think of galleries as commercial establishments and museums as public institutions. However, in Canada the words are often used interchangeably. The gallery took over the old four-story courthouse in 1983, and most of the original building's impressive structure remains. A glass dome over the atrium lets in natural light to soften the imposing building. A large gift shop is located off the main entrance. A childrens' gallery, restaurant and library increase the gallery's popularity. The gallery owns the best collection of Emily Carr, a famous turn-of-the-century British Columbian artist. Admission.

Vancouver Museum. 1100 Chestnut St., Vanier Park (604-341-4604). The pioneer years of British Columbia are emphasized, from the years of exploration through the major immigration period and up to World War I. Among the exhibits are a completely stocked trading post, rail cars and the steerage section from a ship for immigrants. Con-

siderable space is devoted to native cultures. Admission. The **H.R. MacMillan Planetarium** (604-738-7827) next door, has shows each afternoon and evening and rock-music laser-light shows in the evenings. Admission.

Maritime Museum. Vanier Park, near the Vancouver Museum (604-257-8300). The museum's most prized artifact is the *St. Roch*, an RCMP vessel that was the first ship

A few of the many impressive totem ∨ poles in the University of British Columbia's Museum of Anthropology collection.
PROVINCE OF BRITISH COLUMBIA

to sail the Northwest Passage both ways and the first to circumnavigate the North American continent. Several other working vessels are tied up at the museum's Heritage Dock. Bits and pieces of other historical vessels are on display, including parts of the *Beaver*, the first steamship to navigate in the Pacific north of the equator. The re-created salon of the *Empress of India* displays the elegance of steamships in the 1890s, and the forecastle of Capt. George Vancouver's ship *Discovery* has been re-created as well. Admission.

Old Hastings Mill Store Museum. 1575 Alma Road (604-228-1213). The museum, in one of the few buildings to escape the 1886 fire, contains items from the city's history. The mill was the first industrial concern on the south shore of Vancouver. Admission by donation.

Canadian Craft Museum. 639 Hornby St. (604-687-8266). This is the first museum of its kind in Canada. Its permanent exhibits feature knitted clothing and artwork, as well as changing exhibits of national and international traveling shows. Handcrafts are sold in the museum shop. Admission.

Sri Lankan Museum. 925 W. Georgia St., Ste. 150 (604-688-8528). This unusual museum shows gemstones from Sri Lanka and other parts of the world. It is said to be the only museum that deals exclusively in jewels. One of the major pieces is a map of Sri Lanka decorated with precious stones. Admission.

Presentation House. 209 W. 4th St., North Vancouver (604-987-5618). This facility has changing photographic exhibits (admission) and a theater where plays are performed. **North Vancouver Museum and Archives** shares space in the same building. Native and pioneer artifacts are displayed. Free.

Stage Theatres

The City of Vancouver has three theaters under the umbrella of the Vancouver Civic Theatres (VCT): the Queen Elizabeth, the Vancouver Playhouse and the Orpheum. Combined, they have more than 6,000 seats making this the largest civic entertainment complex in Canada. According to the organization, more than 800 events are booked into the theaters each year with over a million people attending performances.

The **Queen Elizabeth Theatre,** at Hamilton and Georgia streets, was opened by Queen Elizabeth II in 1959 and is one of the most popular theaters in North America for visiting companies. It seats 2,937 and hosts Broadway road shows plus ballet performances, operas, pop concerts and special events.

The **Vancouver Playhouse** at Hamilton and Dunsmuir streets, seats 673 and is home to the Vancouver Playhouse Theatre Company, smaller musicals, dance and music recitals. It is ideal for intimate theater and chamber groups.

The **Orpheum,** at Smithe and Seymour, was the largest theater on the Pacific Coast when built in 1927. The city bought it in 1974, restored and refurbished it and reopened it in 1977. The Orpheum seats 2,788 and is home to the Vancouver Symphony Orchestra. Touring orchestral and choral groups, solo recitalists, pop and rock concert artists, solo entertainers appear there.

For information on any of these theaters, call VCT at 604-665-3050. For information on performances and ticket information, check the local newspapers. Tours of the Orpheum, for which a modest fee is charged, are conducted by the Orpheum Heritage Project. Call 604-655-3050 for information.

It is obvious that with these theaters kept so busy, Vancouver enjoys a good reputation for live performances. Several smaller groups perform throughout the city, including:

Arts Club Theatre. 1585 Johnston St., Granville Island (604-687-1644). This is one of the city's most popular theaters. Its two stages feature plays, revues, small musicals and concerts. You can also take in late-night improvisation shows on the weekend.

The Vancouver TheatreSports League. 1100 Chestnut St. (604-688-7013). This group presents improvisational comedy performances at the H.R. MacMillan Planetarium.

Passengers enjoy a panoramic ride on ∧
the cable car that carries them to Grouse
Mountain's observation area.

Waterfront Theatre. Cartwright Street and Old Bridge Street, Granville Island (604-685-6217). Home of the Carousel Theatre which performs family-oriented entertainment.

Musical Organizations

Vancouver Symphony Orchestra. 601 Smithe St. (604-684-9100; Symphony hotline, 876-3434). The symphony is led by conductor Sergiu Comissiona and resident conductor Clyde Mitchell. Ninety concerts are presented each year with the regular season running between October and June. Summer performances are given throughout the region in parks, and even atop Whistler Mountain.

Vancouver Opera. 845 Cambie St. (604-682-2871). The company was formed in 1960 and stages five productions each season. In addition, it sponsors the largest Opera in the Schools Programme in Canada. Performances are given in the Queen Elizabeth Theatre.

Early Music Vancouver. 1254 W. 7th Ave. (604-732-1610). Considered one of the major such groups in the world, Early Music Vancouver offers performances of authentic medieval, renaissance, baroque and early classical music. The concert season runs from autumn through spring. Additional concerts are given throughout the summer along with workshops for students and amateur musicians from all over the world.

Uzume Taiko. 100-1062 Homer St. (604-683-8240). The first professional taiko (Japanese drumming) group in Canada, Uzume Taiko has earned an international reputation from its tours of Europe and North America.

VANCOUVER HOTELS

Vancouver has come into its own in the hotel business in recent years and has some of the best hotels in the Evergreen Triangle: both the American Automobile Association and the Canadian Automobile Association have given the city three five-star hotels—the Four Seasons Hotel, Le Meridien and the Pan Pacific. Several others have earned four-star ratings. By comparison, Seattle has only one five-star (the Four Seasons Olympic) and Victoria none. Unfortunately, most of central Vancouver's hotels are quite expensive; an exception is the Sylvia. To find a good moderate-priced hotel you will have to stay on the outskirts of town, in North or West Vancouver or south toward Richmond.

Code: Inexpensive – $60 and less; Moderate – $60 to $100. Expensive – $100 and up.

Avalon Motor Hotel, 1025 Marine Dr., North Vancouver (604-985-4181). This small motel, with 30 units, is convenient to the SeaBus that runs between Lonsdale Quay at North Vancouver and downtown. Five of its rooms have whirlpools, and a restaurant is attached. *Moderate.*

Best Western Capilano Inn, 1634 Capilano Rd., North Vancouver (604-987-8185). This is a good location for seeing North and West Vancouver without worrying about the slow traffic across the Lions Gate Bridge, especially when you plan to take B.C. Rail north or to catch an early ferry out of Horseshoe Bay. It has 71 units, some with mountain views. *Inexpensive off-season, moderate in summer.*

Four Seasons Hotel, 791 W. Georgia St. (604-689-9333). This is one of Vancouver's best hotels, in spite of a strange, cramped entrance that makes it look like a shopping plaza. Once you take the escalator to the reception area, everything changes for the better. Its lobby is spacious and has interesting artwork, discreet shops, a small, pleasant bar and, during the Christmas holiday season, trees decorated by local businesses. Its 385 units include numerous suites, rooms in several configurations and all the amenities: massages, health club, business center, pool, sauna, whirlpool. *Expensive.*

Hotel Georgia, 801 W. Georgia St. (604-682-5566). This is another of those old-fashioned hotels that predate the glass and fern lobbies and offer anonymity as well as a good place to sleep. The lobby is small and the rooms larger than many newer hotels. The restaurant is just okay, but many fine restaurants and some of the best downtown shopping are within walking distance. *Expensive.*

Granville Island Hotel and Marina, 1253 Johnston St. (604-683-7373). This hotel is something of a puzzlement because it must be the noisiest hotel in Canada when the band is cranked up in the disco. But its Granville Island location is unbeatable—right on the water with great views of the city and mountains. A marina is attached where you can sign up for charters or rent boats or kayaks. *Expensive.*

Lonsdale Quay Hotel, 123 Carrie Cates Court, North Vancouver (604-986-6111). This unusual hotel is part of the popular Lonsdale Quay Market at the foot of Lonsdale, and the terminal for the SeaBus. The hotel has 57 units, each with good views of the harbor and mountains. *Expensive.*

Le Meridien, 845 Burrard St. (604-682-5511). Probably Vancouver's most luxurious hotel, if not of the entire Evergreen Triangle. Its French provincial furnishings are the kind you would expect in the home of a European industrialist with good taste. It has thick carpets throughout, silk bedspreads, marble bathrooms, a formal dining room and the Cafe Fleuri with its chocolate buffet on Fridays and Saturdays and Sunday brunch. *Expensive.*

O'Doul's Hotel, 1300 Robson St. (604-684-8461). A pleasant hotel with airy rooms in the heart of the Robson Street shopping area, within easy walking distance of the downtown area or Stanley Park. The hotel has 130 units, restaurant, pool and good views. *Expensive.*

Pan Pacific, 999 Canada Place (604-662-8111). This large (505 units) hotel extends into Coal Harbour and is part of the Canada Place cruise ship terminal and Convention Centre. In spite of the obvious attraction for conventions, the hotel can provide almost everything you would want. Its rooms have stunning views of the city, inlet and mountains, and its health club is one of the best you'll find anywhere. It is an easy walk to Gastown and anywhere else downtown. *Expensive.*

Park Royal Hotel, 540 Clyde Ave., West Vancouver (604-926-5511). This is one of the favorite places for people preferring to stay on the edge of Vancouver rather than downtown. The 30-unit hotel overlooks the Capilano River and is near a large shopping complex. The West Vancouver seawall walk begins nearby and a pathway also leads north along the river. The hotel is near the Lions Gate Bridge and on the main route to Highway 1. *Expensive.*

Sylvia Hotel, 1154 Guilford St. (604-681-9321). This small (115 rooms) hotel on English Bay is a particular favorite among Seattleites who go to Vancouver for a romantic weekend. So far it has remained unaffected by all the high-rise activity around it, giving the impression that its ivy-covered walls will stand for a long time to come. Its rooms aren't always elegant; some of them are a bit on the threadbare side and some of its carpets are worn beyond belief. But it is in such a nice location and the staff is so relaxed and personable that you don't care. A light and airy restaurant with floor to ceiling windows overlooks English Bay. Some corner suites are available with kitchens. *Moderate.*

Hotel Vancouver, 900 W. Georgia St. (604-684-3131). If you're looking for one of those old-fashioned hotels with a large lobby, excellent restaurant, pleasant and unobtrusive service, and a convenient location, this elderly but well-maintained hotel will make you feel comfortable. It has 508 units and 42 suites, three restaurants and two lounges. *Expensive.*

Waterfront Centre Hotel, 900 Canada Pl. (604-691-1991). Directly across the street from the Pan Pacific and the cruise terminal, this relatively new hotel is tied to Canada Place with an underground shopping mall. It has 489 rooms and a concierge level with its own staff, café and bar. The views are almost as spectacular as from the Pan Pacific. Very convenient location. *Expensive.*

Westin Bayshore, 1601 W. Georgia St. (604-682-3377). This beautiful property is right on the water at the edge of Stanley Park. It consists of a low-rise building with a tower next to it. (It was here on the top floor that the late American industrialist Howard Hughes holed up for several months.) Other amenities include both indoor and outdoor pools, a boat basin with charter boats and moorage for private boats or seaplanes, and a large garden. Its most popular restaurant is Trader Vic's. The Sunday brunch in the main restaurant is popular with non-guests. *Expensive.*

Bed and Breakfasts

As with elsewhere in North America, several Vancouverites have turned their homes into bed and breakfasts. One of the major booking agencies, with nearly 40 B&Bs for clients, is Town & Country Bed & Breakfast, Box 74542, 2803 W. Fourth Ave. (604-731-5942). The prices range from $65 for shared bathroom to $150.

Airport Hotels

Best Western Abercorn Inn, 9260 Bridgeport Rd., Richmond (604-270-7576). Only 2.5 miles (4 km) from the airport, this motel, with 79 units, is styled as a Scottish country inn. Ten rooms have whirlpools. *Moderate.*

Coast Vancouver Airport Hotel, 1041 S.W. Marine Dr. (604-263-1555). A pleasant place to stay 2.5 miles (4 km) from the airport. Sauna, whirlpool and exercise room with a restaurant attached. *Moderate.*

Delta Town and Country Inn, 6005 Highway 17, Delta (604-946-4404). This 48-unit country motel is 7.5 miles

< *The moon appears suspended over Vancouver's Canada Place.*
Tourism Vancouver

(12 km) from the Tsawwassen ferry dock. A restaurant, tennis courts and heated pool. *Moderate.*

Quality Inn, 725 S.E. Marine Dr. (604-321-6611). Only 3 miles (5 km) from the airport, this 100-unit motel has a restaurant but few other amenities. *Inexpensive.*

RV Parks

Capilano RV Park, 295 Tomahawk Ave., North Vancouver (604-987-4722), is right in town and convenient to the Lions Gate Bridge. Open all year.

Parkcanada RV Inns, 4799 Hwy. 17, Delta (604-943-5811), is near the ferry terminal and next door to the Splashdown Waterslide Park.

....

VANCOUVER RESTAURANTS

 Not so many years ago Vancouver wasn't a particularly exciting place to dine. Like the other cities in the Evergreen Triangle, it had the usual "Continental" fare, the restaurants in Chinatown, and an occasional good neighborhood Italian or German restaurant. Things have changed since the 1960s, and it has been estimated that it would take six years to eat dinner in each of Vancouver's more than 2,000 restaurants. Many of us would like to try.

You can have Chinese food from virtually every province in that vast land. You can enjoy the cuisine of Thailand, Cambodia, Vietnam, Korea, Japan, Indonesia, Malaysia, Australia (even!), New Zealand, India, Hawaii, Northwest Coast, Britain, Ireland, France, Italy, Germany, Scandinavia, Greece, Turkey, the Middle East, North Africa... the list goes on and on.

You can also have the so-called Northwest Cuisine, which is perhaps a bit over-named. Northwest Cuisine is mainly fresh local food, including such seafood as salmon, cod, Dungeness crab, shrimp and local fresh fruit, berries and vegetables. It is good food, to be sure, but to call it a cuisine may be stretching the limits of accuracy.

With all of this to consider, making a list of restaurants is not an enviable chore. However, those listed here have been in business awhile and are some of the most popular. It is always a good idea to check with the concierge or front desk in your hotel before committing yourself to an expensive dinner.

Code: *Inexpensive – $10 or less per person; Moderate – $10 to $20; Expensive – Over $30.*

First, a small selection of the ethnic restaurants:

African

The **Kilimanjaro** at 332 Water St. (604-681-9913), in the heart of Gastown, has a menu that includes baked trout, yams and cucumber soup. *Inexpensive.*

Nyala Ethiopian Restaurant at 2930 West 4th Ave. (604-731-7899), is another popular African restaurant. Ethiopian food is eaten without utensils. Instead, a flat bread is torn into pieces and used to scoop up the food. *Inexpensive.*

Chinese

One of the delights of Chinatown is going there for dim sum, a combination of breakfast and lunch—brunch if you will—that is served in numerous restaurants. My travel writer friend and guidebook writer Carol Baker says it is best to sit close to the kitchen so you'll have first choice of the items that come out on trays to make the rounds. She recommends the **Flamingo**, 3469 Fraser St. (604-887-1231), the **Pink Pearl**, 1132 Hastings St. (604-253-4316); **Mings**, 147 East Pender St. (604-683-4722), and **Maxim's Bakery**, 257 Keefer St. (604-688-6281). For dinner she recommends the **Won More**, 1184 Denman St. (604-688-8856, and **Tai Chi Hin** at 888 Burrard St. (604-682-1888). *All are inexpensive.*

French

Le Crocodile, 909 Burrard St. (604-669-4298), is one of Vancouver's most popular French restaurants. *Expensive.*

Le Gavroche, 1616 Alberni St. (604-685-3924), is a more intimate restaurant in a converted home with a view across

Coal Harbour. Daily specials are featured. It is noted for seafood. *Expensive.*

Greek

Simpatico Ristorante, 222 W. 4th Ave. (604-733-6824). This is one of the most reasonably priced restaurants in the city, as generations of students have discovered. Pizza is a favorite, and each table has its own pizza stand. *Inexpensive.*

The Greek Connection, 1560 Marine Dr., West Vancouver (604-926-4228), is another good buy. Many locals grumbled when its hole-in-the-wall look was modernized, but the menu remained the same, and so did the price. *Moderate.*

Greek Characters Restaurant, 1 Alexander St. (604-681-6581). This is a popular place for Gastown visitors. It serves Greek dishes, seafood, burgers and steaks. *Moderate.*

Italian

Umberto's is a chain with restaurants throughout the city. The best-known is **Umberto Al Porto** at 321 Water St. (604-683-8376), in Gastown. The large restaurant has two levels with good views across Coal Harbour. *Moderate.*

Masked Haida dancers perform ∧
traditional dances before a
reconstructed longhouse.
TOURISM VANCOUVER

Japanese

There are several throughout the city, most in the expensive category, such as **Koji Japanese Restaurant,** 630 Hornby St. (604-685-7355), and **Restaurant Suntory,** Pan Pacific Hotel, 999 Canada Place Way (604-683-8201).

Kamei Sushi, 1030 W. Georgia St. (604-687-8588), offers sushi, miso soup, teriyaki, tempura, yakitori and numerous other popular Japanese dishes. Also has take-out. *Moderate.*

Kakiemon, 200 Burrard St. (604-688-6866). Located in the Waterfront Centre office building next to Canada Place, this is one of the city's most elegant Japanese restaurants. The menu includes sunomono, tempura, udon, robata, sushi and seafood from the tank. *Expensive.*

Native

Quilicum Restaurant, 1724 Davie St. (604-681-7044). The interior of a cedar longhouse has been recreated with tables at ground level and your feet in pits. Food served in alder bowls consists of smoked fish, barbecued goat ribs, oolichan (candlefish), duck, and various plants such as fern shoots, dried seaweed, and soapberries for dessert. *Moderate.*

Spanish

La Bodega, 1277 Howe St. (604-684-8815). This is a popular gathering spot for those with an interest in things Spanish. It is a casual, friendly place that serves traditional Spanish food, including plates of patatas bravas and tapas. *Moderate.*

Vietnamese

Vina Restaurant, 851 Denman St. (604-688-3232). This is one of the best places to sample the food that reflects the Orient as well as the years Vietnam was a French colony. *Inexpensive.*

The following restaurants were selected in part for their location, meaning they have good views or are in a particularly interesting location.

The Beachside, 1362 Marine Dr., West Vancouver (604-925-1945). A good view of English Bay with both inside and outside dining. *Moderate.*

The Cannery, 2205 Commissioner St. (604-254-9606), specializes in seafood, which makes sense since the popular spot uses the theme of coast commercial fishing in its decor. *Moderate*

The English Bay Boathouse corner of Denman and Beach streets (604-669-2225), has a sweeping view across the strip of park along Beach Drive and English Bay. Specializes in fresh sea food; also offers barbecued meats. You can sit on the view deck in good weather. *Moderate.*

The Old Spaghetti Factory, 53 Water St., Gastown (604-684-1288). Yes, you'll find this favorite in Vancouver, and when you're traveling with children or relatives who don't want a dining experience, just food, this is the place to go. *Inexpensive.*

The Prow Restaurant, 999 Canada Place, Ste. 100 (604-684-1339), features Northwest cuisine with seafood a specialty. Waterfront views and patio dining, weather permitting, are among its features. *Expensive.*

Salmon House on the Hill, 2229 Folkestone Way, West Vancouver (604-926-3212), offers panoramic views of the city with its specialty of barbecued salmon. *Moderate.*

The Ship of the Seven Seas, foot of Lonsdale in North Vancouver (604-987-3344), is a floating restaurant at the Lonsdale Quay. It is well known for its seafood buffet. *Expensive.*

Sylvia's, Sylvia Hotel, Beach and Gilford streets (604-681-9321), is a pleasant place for brunch or dinner with its great views across English Bay and friendly staff. *Moderate.*

The Teahouse, Ferguson Point in Stanley Park (604-669-3281). One of Vancouver's institutions, The Teahouse has such a nice setting in the woods with a view that you may not think about the food, which is certainly acceptable. *Moderate.*

Tudor Room, Park Royal Hotel, 540 Clyde Ave., West Vancouver (604-926-5511), offers regional foods in season, including seafood, wild game and steaks. *Moderate.*

The William Tell, Georgian Court Hotel, 773 Beatty St. (604-688-3504), features Swiss and French menus. The restaurant, one of Vancouver's most expensive, enforces a dress code.

Nightlife

As you would expect in such a vibrant city, Vancouver has a lively nightlife. Clubs are scattered through Granville Island, in the downtown core, and in most large hotels. Clubs open and close, and they change their type of bands and entertainment. Thus, it is best to check with your concierge or to pick up a copy of the *Vancouver Sun* or the *Georgia Straight* for the latest information.

Here is a brief selection of nightclubs:

Big Bam Boo Club, 1236 W. Broadway (604-733-2220). Live dance bands plus disco, light show and a sushi bar.

Richards on Richards, 1036 Richards St. (604-687-6794). A popular spot for young adults. Upscale decor, taped and live (weekends) top-40 bands.

Shenanigan's on Robson, 1225 Robson St. (604-688-1411). A large pub with a wide screen video for sporting events and a dance floor with a DJ and the top 40 tunes.

If you just want a drink and a place to talk, try any hotel in the downtown area. Nearly all have a lounge or a pub. You may have better luck finding a quiet bar in British Columbia than in Washington. Bar owners in the Seattle area seem to get fidgety if they don't have music loud enough to give you a toothache.

A jazz quartet enlivens >
Victoria's waterfront across
from the Parliament Buildings.
Province of British Columbia

Victoria

Selkirk Water

Bay St.

Esquimalt Rd.

West Bay

Shoal Pt.

Laure

Victoria Harbour

Canadian Coast Guard

St. Lawrence St.

Breakwater

N

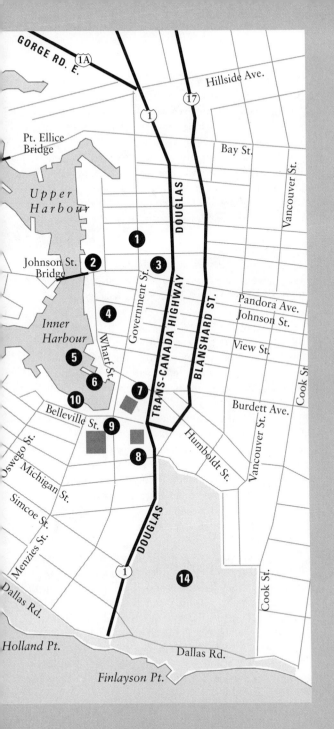

GORGE RD. E.

1A

Hillside Ave.

17

1

Pt. Ellice
Bridge

Bay St.

*Upper
Harbour*

DOUGLAS

Johnson St.
Bridge

2

1

3

Government St.

Vancouver St.

*Inner
Harbour*

4

Pandora Ave.
Johnson St.

TRANS-CANADA HIGHWAY

BLANSHARD ST.

View St.

5

Wharf St.

6

Cook St.

10

7

Burdett Ave.

Belleville St.

9

Vancouver St.

Oswego St.

Michigan St.

8

Humboldt St.

Cook St.

Simcoe St.

Menzies St.

DOUGLAS

Dallas Rd.

1

14

Cook St.

Holland Pt.

Dallas Rd.

Finlayson Pt.

Victoria, British Columbia's capital, is an anomaly, a time warp, a Brigadoon that stays, a Victorian England that never really existed. Mostly, it is an exercise in nostalgia for something few of us have ever known. In a region best known for its outdoor activities, its casual clothing and unpretentiousness, there sits Victoria in all its formal, precise grandeur amid its acres of flowers tended by retired British couples who wear coats and ties and dresses whether they expect company or not. Afternoon tea is not an occasion for them; it is the mother's milk of civilization.

In all fairness, that paragraph is slightly exaggerated. While Seattle feels threatened by Southern Californians and Vancouverites sometimes feel a bridge has been built from Hong Kong to Pender Street, Victorians are stuck with the image of retired Brits mired in their rigid social structure and no-more-new-taxes attitudes. However, the facts don't support the clichés here, either. In fact, very few Victorian newcomers are from the UK; most are from British Columbia, but the information we choose to believe is frequently more interesting than the truth, or at least more dramatic.

Victoria is the largest of the towns around the Evergreen Triangle that have a theme look, or at least a cultural connection with another country. Victoria is also one of the most honest because it has always been what it is today. The townsite was selected for the excellent harbor which winds around for several miles through town. And once the harbor was discovered, so was that magnificent climate, some say the most pleasing climate in all of North America.

Victoria's downtown area reflects the British heritage that brings the city so much tourism money. The shops are heavy on United Kingdom and British Commonwealth products: woolen clothing and tartans from Scotland; china from England; brass items from India; Inuit artwork from the Canadian north; sweaters, moccasins, masks and beadwork from British Columbia natives.

Visitors love it, and every day the year around they arrive on ferries, tour boats, airplanes, busses and automobiles.

In the summer the number runs in the thousands per day. Many arrive on day trips from Vancouver and Washington's Olympic Peninsula. Others you see on the street are there to spend several days or a week in the area. Tourism in Victoria is a giant industry. A few years ago one study showed that it had the largest per-capita tourist trade in all of Canada, including Quebec City.

This small city has one of the most beautiful marine settings in the world. Added to the scenery is a scattering of small offshore islands in Discovery Island Marine Park. Victoria's stone public buildings were constructed for both show and for durability; they look as though they could ride out an earthquake, a hurricane or a modest war. The government buildings along the Inner Harbour are further dramatized each night when hundreds of thousands of light bulbs outline the massive buildings and the nearby Empress Hotel built in the same style.

Because of its quaintness, its lack of big-city stress, its safe streets and the overall feeling of remoteness, Victoria is for most visitors the most romantic of the three cities. And it has a wonderful climate; in fact, the Gonzales Observatory in Victoria is the only official weather station in Canada to have gone an entire winter without recording snowfall.

Thus, Victoria is the warmest city in Canada during the winter and the coolest and driest in the summer with more hours of sunshine than any other Canadian city (2,196 compared with Vancouver's 1,925 hours). Its frost-free season normally lasts eight months, the longest in Canada, which helps explain the Victorian passion for gardening.

In 1937, the city was the first in the Evergreen Triangle to display hanging baskets of flowers. The baskets were so popular that each year, between June and September, the floral baskets are hung from lamp standards throughout the downtown and Inner Harbour area. In December the parks department plants seeds in the baskets; and each has 25 plants. In May the public is invited to the greenhouses to admire the 600 or more baskets before they go onto the lamp standards. Every night street cleaners and sweepers descend on the downtown core, keeping it perhaps the cleanest of any city its size (70,000) in North America.

Parliament Buildings

501 Belleville St. (Call the tour coordinator at 604-387-3046). The Parliament Buildings, along with the Empress Hotel, dominate the skyline along the Inner Harbour. The buildings were designed by a local architect named Francis Rattenbury in a mixture of Victorian, Roman and Italian Renaissance styles, and were completed in 1897. The façade's outline is illuminated by more than 3,300 small light bulbs fixed along the corners of the walls, a feature that has contributed to the buildings' landmark status. They were first turned on to celebrate Queen Victoria's Diamond Jubilee in 1912.

Stationed along the sides of the buildings are statues of various historical figures: Capt. George Vancouver, first European to sail around the island named in his honor; Sir James Douglas, founder and first governor of Victoria, and Sir Matthew Baillie Begbie, chief law enforcer during the province's early years. Queen Victoria's statue stands in front of the buildings facing the harbor.

In 1973, restoration work began that extended from the

Previous Pages:
*A quiet scene in Victoria's
Beacon Hill Park.*
PROVINCE OF BRITISH COLUMBIA

*Butchart Gardens, once a ∧
quarry, now a glorious year-
round ornamental display.*
BUTCHART GARDENS

foundations to the statue of George Vancouver on top of the central dome. Stained glass windows were repaired. Moldings, light fixtures and door knobs were made to replicate the originals, and mosaic tiles and ornate plaster work were restored. After ten years of work, the buildings were returned to their earlier magnificence. Free guided tours of the buildings are available for groups and in half a dozen languages. Large groups must phone ahead.

Butchart Gardens

800 Benvenuto Ave., Brentwood (604-652-5256). Most people mention Victoria and Butchart Gardens in the same breath. Although they are 10 miles (16 km) north of Victoria near Brentwood on Tod Inlet, they have become synonymous with the city for most visitors.

Butchart Gardens cover 50 acres (20 ha) set in the remnants of a wooded limestone quarry abandoned in the early part of the 20th century. Within them are individual theme gardens—the English Rose Garden, Japanese and Italian gardens, and the Sunken Garden with its dancing fountain. The gardens are immaculate no matter what time of the year you go. During July and August regular stage shows, fireworks displays and daily entertainment are scheduled. Tour busses bring visitors from downtown Victoria. Moorage is available for private yachts sailing in via scenic Saanich Inlet. Admission.

Butterfly Gardens

1461 Benvenuto Ave. (604-652-3822). While you're in the Butchart Gardens neighborhood, you may want to stop at this newer attraction. The first Butterfly World was opened near Parksville, north of Nanaimo, and was such a success that this one followed a short time later. Butterflies from Asia, the Americas, Africa and other parts of the world are reared at special farms and then brought to Butterfly World to live out their lives. Some species are threatened by extinction as their natural habitat—tropical rainforests—are cleared. You can see all stages of butterflies' lives here, from breeding through egg laying, caterpillar rearing and so forth. Admission.

Crystal Gardens

713 Douglas St. (604-381-1213). Located behind the Empress Hotel, this glass-domed complex has a little bit of a lot of different things: a saltwater swimming pool (the largest in the British Empire when it was built in 1925); a small zoo of tropical creatures—pygmy marmosets, flamingoes, macaws, tropical penguins, wallabies, squirrels, iguanas and tropical fish, plants and various other birds and fish from the South Pacific.

It is also a shopping mall with an emphasis on artwork by regional artists, jewelry, and gift items from other British Commonwealth countries.

Each day English tea is served on the promenade, in the English fashion. Weddings, craft fairs and other special events are often held in the garden. Admission.

Craigdarroch Castle

1050 Joan Crescent (604-592-5323). Robert Dunsmuir, one of Victoria's first coal barons, believed that a man's home should be his castle, so in the 1880s he built one of British Columbia's most lavish houses. Unfortunately, he died before the castle was finished. His widow Joan moved into Craigdarroch in 1890 and lived there until she died in 1908.

Craigdarroch is now a museum furnished in turn-of-the-century style; many of the pieces are the originals. The castle has been restored and features magnificent stained glass windows, intricately carved oak panelling on the walls and ceiling of the main hall, walnut, mahogany, cedar and spruce panelling in many of the rooms, and complex designs executed in exotic wood in the parquet floor throughout the castle's 39 rooms. Admission.

VIA Rail's Malahat Route

Old Vancouver Island hands still call it the E&N, the Esquimalt and Nanaimo Railway, but it has been a VIA Rail route for several years. The 140-mile (225-km) railroad uses self-propelled RDCs, rail diesel cars with the engine in the front of one car.

The train leaves the station at 450 Pandora Avenue daily

at 8:15 A.M. and returns at 5:45 P.M., making it a full day's trip with time for a good breakfast before leaving and a good dinner after returning. The train's schedule shows more than two dozen stops, but many of those are flag stops only. You can take your own lunch or jump off at Nanaimo at 10:40 A.M., have lunch then re-board when the train returns. Courtney is the end of the line. The train arrives there at 12:50 P.M. and leaves for Victoria at 1:15 P.M. If you buy your ticket seven days in advance from VIA or a travel agency, you get a 40% discount. No phone reservations taken. 1-800-561-8630.

Special Places

Victoria has more of a European look than most cities in Western Canada, and its quaint squares—Bastion Square, Market Square, Chinatown—are part of the reason.

The squares and small streets all have a history and atmosphere, one of the reasons you should walk through the main district. Victoria is basically a small city, and except for the evening rush hour, you'll find walking always a pleasure.

Bastion Square. This popular square, just off Wharf Street, is the original site of Fort Victoria, established by its first governor, James Douglas, in 1843. The original courthouse and several other turn-of-the-century buildings surrounding the square have been restored and currently house gift shops, restaurants and offices. The **Maritime Museum,** in the old courthouse, contains a large collection of ship models, scrimshaw, a model of a paddlewheel steamer, and many bits and pieces of ships that sailed in the area.

Chinatown. This neighborhood once covered several city blocks but is now centered on Fisgard Street. At one time more than 8,000 workers imported from the China's Pearl River Delta lived in the area, but over the years Vancouver became the Port of Entry for immigrants, and Victoria's Chinatown declined. It now covers about two square blocks between Pandora Street on the south and Herald Street on the north. Store Street is the western boundary and Government Street is more or less the eastern boundary.

Off to the side is **Fan Tan Alley,** called Canada's narrowest street, a slit of a passage with several shops and artists' retail outlets. On Fisgard, the ornate, red Gate of Harmonious Interest leads to dozens of shops that sell Oriental goods. Several Chinese restaurants are found in the district.

The unique district was given a new life when the city government invested public funds in a restoration program that included Chinese lamp posts, bilingual street signs and construction of the Gate of Harmonious Interest.

Market Square. This award-winning mall, on Johnson and Store streets, began its life as a packhouse and busy warehouse when gold was discovered in B.C.'s interior. It now consists of a collection of small shops—more than 40 in fact—surrounding a central courtyard. Jazz festivals are held each summer in the courtyard.

Beacon Hill Park. This hilltop park is a brisk walk from downtown, and worth the effort. It owes its existence to the Hudson's Bay Company, which set the area aside as a park and named it for the navigational beacons placed on it in the 1840s. In addition to its great views of the Olympic Peninsula and the British Columbia mainland, the park features gardens, duck ponds, a small farm zoo, lawn bowling and picnic areas. It even has a cricket field, where curious Americans—and many Canadians—can watch and wonder at this game that is a national passion in England and almost never played in North America. The park was selected as Mile 0 of the Trans-Canada highway, which officially begins its 5,000-mile (8047 km) journey to the Atlantic here.

Miniature World. Empress Hotel, 649 Humbolt St. (604-385-9731). This collection is one of Victoria's most unusual visitor attractions; the more time you spend going through the exhibits, the larger you feel. The collection includes battle scenes from European and North American history, various cities at different stages of their past (Quebec City in 1910, for example), a tiny sawmill that actually works, several fairy tales come to life, an entire circus, the Great Canadian Railway in 1885, a space station from 2201, for a total of 80 subjects. Admission.

Two of the most popular tours of Victoria are by horse-drawn carriage and aboard a tiny boat:

The Tallyho (604-479-1113) has been a Victoria fixture since 1903, and its popularity continues. You are taken through the city on a rubber-tired wagon drawn by a team of horses. The (summer-only) tour includes a swing around the harbor, through Thunderbird Park and up to the summit of Beacon Hill Park. The return route is via James Bay with its expensive homes. The same company also offers **Black Beauty Carriage Tours,** single horse-drawn carriages for up to six people. All-year; phone 604-361-1220.

Victoria Harbour Ferry Company. This company operates the small, covered boats you will see putt-putting around the harbor. The boats run on two routes, both originating at the main harbor dock directly in front of the Empress. One route runs west to the Esquimalt Peninsula at Songhees Park and West Bay, and back across to Fisherman's Wharf and Coast Harbourside. The other route runs to Chinatown, Point Ellice, Banfield Park and Gorge Park. You can make reservations through your hotel or the Tourism Victoria Infocentre at the Inner Harbour.

VICTORIA HOTELS

Vancouver and Seattle may have more five-diamond hotels, and they may have a wider selection than Victoria, but they don't have the Empress. Only Victoria has that architectural masterpiece, and it is so overpowering that it can't be ignored. You may want to stay in a more modern hotel, or one that is more intimate, but you will at least want to walk through it, whether you stay there or not. Actually, Victoria has numerous hotels, inns and B&Bs, and it isn't fair to them to think only of the Empress when Victoria is mentioned. But that is the way it seems to work out for most visitors.

Three Victoria hotels preserve the wonderful English-style Christmas tradition: the Empress, Olde England Inn and Oak Bay Beach Hotel.

Code: Inexpensive – $60 or less; Moderate – $60 to $100; Expensive – $100 and up.

The Empress, 721 Government St. (604-384-8111). The hotel's brochures say that Victoria is the Empress and the Empress is Victoria. It is true: This 482-room landmark competes with Butchart Gardens as the city's symbol for visitors. It was designed by the same Francis Mawson Rattenbury, who designed the legislative buildings, and was

A British Christmas in the New World

A Christmas parade led by young men carrying a boar's head on a silver platter may not sound like an inviting way to begin Christmas dinner, but when the boar's head is made of plastic and the event is held in a Victoria hotel, the result is both Old World charm and New World sentimentality.

Christmas "grete feasts" are an English tradition first brought to British Columbia by employees of the Hudson's Bay Company and nurtured over the years.

Not surprisingly, this traditional English cus-tom has been adopted in Victoria, one of those British colonial cities scattered around the world that are "more British than Britain." Three hotels in Victoria are best known for these Christmas feasts: The Empress, Olde England Inn and the Oak Bay. Each hotel has its own character and attracts a different clientele. Thus, the venerable Empress Hotel, Victoria's major landmark on the Inner Harbour and a bastion of British civility, attracts a large number of elderly, sedate, retired British civil servants as holiday guests. High tea is served daily in the enormous lobby near the towering Christmas built with 30-inch (76-cm)-thick walls sturdy enough to withstand a war.

Everyone seems to have stayed there, including the British royal family from time to time and many actors and actresses. Richard and Pat Nixon spent their honeymoon there. It had only 116 rooms when it opened in 1908. Two years later the north wing and library were added. (The library is now the Bengal Lounge.) This still wasn't enough space, so in 1929 another 270 rooms were added on Humboldt Street, and a new wing has been added recently.

As newer hotels were built, guests loyal to the Empress

tree while carolers sing from the staircase. It is one of those events visitors treasure almost as much as the Christmas feast itself.

The Olde England Inn is modeled after a medieval baronial hall with rich, dark paneling and rooms decorated in authentic period furniture and named for royalty of the era.

Oak Bay Beach Hotel is removed from the hustle and bustle of downtown Victoria, and consequently has the air of a neighborhood residence. In fact, many people from the neighborhood make the hotel bar their gathering place. It isn't unusual for guests to form friend-ships with locals.

All hotels offer similar Christmas feasts of five to seven courses, served amid much pomp and caroling. It is the programs surrounding the feast that differ, but in all cases, the feast is interspersed with entertainers — carolers, soloists and, at the Olde England Inn, a magician who is a something of a bumbler. It is uncertain if his awkwardness is part of the act or just his normal style.

Reservations are essential. Christmas feasts have become so popular that some hotels offering the two- or three-day package are booked nearly a year in advance.

needed a sense of humor because the elderly hotel had no air conditioning nor an adequate heating system. In 1966 a renovation project that cost $45 million brought it into the present. Luxury suites were added, and the honeymoon suites on the seventh floor, called the Attic, were redecorated, as were all other rooms. The lobby area was expanded to include an indoor pool and recreation pavilion with views of the harbor.

The entire building verges on overstatement, but in a sedate rather than ostentatious manner. The 11-foot (3.65-m) wide corridors are decorated with antique furniture and lined with portraits of royalty and of the wives of Canada's Governors General. Ceilings are so high that you couldn't see cobwebs even if they were there. The Crystal Ballroom has a maze of crystal chandeliers. The temptation of writers is to go on and on, as I am, but this gives you an idea of what to expect in one of the top four or five historic hotels in North America. *Expensive.*

∧ *The Empress Hotel is one of Canada's most beloved institutions.*
EMPRESS HOTEL

Admiral Motel, 257 Belleville St. (604-388-6267). This is one of the best buys in Victoria: a harbor view in a quiet area. The rooms were recently renovated, and 23 of the 29 units have kitchen facilities. *Moderate.*

The Bedford, 1140 Government St. (604-384-6835). This European-style hotel in the heart of the shopping district is one of the most popular among visitors who prefer privacy over great views or opulence. Several of the 40 rooms have their own fireplaces and whirlpools. It also has a restaurant. *Expensive.*

Best Western Inner Harbour, 412 Quebec St. (604-384-5122). This apartment hotel is right on the harbor and each large unit has a balcony. All but two of the 74 units have kitchens. Pool, sauna and whirlpool. *Moderate.*

Chateau Victoria, 740 Burdett Ave. (604-382-4221). One of the nicer downtown motels with 178 units, 7 two-room suites and 13 with kitchens. Heated pool and whirlpool. Restaurant and cocktail lounge on the property. *Expensive.*

Cheltenham Court Motel, 994 Gorge Rd. (604-385-9559). If you don't mind being a short distance 2 miles (5 km) from the center of town, this is a good place to stay at a low price. The motel has several duplex cottages and housekeeping units on extensive grounds with views across the ocean inlet. *Inexpensive.*

The Coachman Inn, 229 Gorge Road E. (604-388-6611). Located 1.2 miles (2 km) northwest of the downtown area, this Tudor-style motel has 12 small (one-bedroom) housekeeping units in addition to the 62 motel units. A restaurant serves three meals daily. It also has a cocktail lounge. *Moderate.*

Crystal Court Motel, 701 Belleville St. (604-384-0551). This unpretentious and modestly priced motel features a convenient location—only four blocks from the Empress and near the bus station and Beacon Hill Park. It has 57 units with refrigerators and free parking. *Inexpensive.*

Oak Bay Beach Hotel, 1175 Beach Dr. (604-598-4556). This Tudor-style hotel is far from the downtown crowds and on the east side of what is called the Tweed Curtain, a description of the neighborhoods that separate the commercial aspects of Victoria from the genteel village of Oak Bay. The hotel has 51 rooms, a cozy and very popular pub that draws many local customers—it may remind you of a British version of "Cheers"—and an excellent restaurant, the Oak Room, with grand saltwater views. The hotel's own yacht is used for tours of the area and fishing charters. During the Christmas season it is used for tours showing the city's Christmas lighting. Across the street is an excellent golf course, and Beach Drive is a good route for biking, jogging or walking. *Expensive.*

Ocean Pointe Resort, 45 Songhees Rd. (604-360-2999). This 250-room chateau-style hotel is the newest addition to Victoria's harbor and gives customers grandstand views of the waterfront activity and the parliament buildings. Among its features are a European-style spa with hydrotherapy, sauna, aroma therapy and a full range of beauty treatments. It has two lighted tennis courts, a racquetball court and an indoor pool. *Expensive.*

Olde England Inn, 429 Lampson St. (604-388-4353). This is the kind of place pseudo-sophisticates aren't supposed to like, but usually do. The hotel has 55 rooms, many with woodburning fireplaces and most decorated with some of the most impressive antiques you'll find in Victoria. One time I stayed in the King of Portugal Room and slept in a canopied bed once owned by King John VI. (He was a very short man.) The hotel's restaurant, the Shakespeare Dining Room, serves English-style food (Yorkshire pudding, trifle, crumpets and scones are prominent on the menu) and candlelit dinners.

The hotel and restaurant are only part of the attraction. The complex has several other buildings, all reminders of something back home in England. (The founders of Olde England Inn came to the colony from Yorkshire.) A replica of William Shakespeare's birthplace stands on the grounds as part of the English village, along with Anne Hathaway's cottage. The Inn's brochure points out that daily tours are conducted by "Tudor wenches." *Moderate to expensive.*

Swan's Hotel and Pub, 506 Pandora Ave. (604-361-3310). This building began as a feed store and granary, then became a 29-room B&B hotel with a working brewery on the lower level. Most of the accommodations are two-story suites with two bedrooms and fully equipped kitchens. Breakfast is delivered to the door each morning. The café serves lunch and dinner, and the pub has pipes directly from the brewery to the tap. Tours of the brewery are part of the package. *Expensive.*

Bed and Breakfasts

Heritage House B&B, 3808 Heritage Lane. (604-479-0892). One of the nicer B&Bs, 3 miles (5 km) from downtown. The five non-smoking units share three bathrooms. A wrap-around porch is a great place for visiting or just sitting. A two-night minimum stay is required as are reservations. No children under 12. Gourmet breakfasts are served. *Moderate.*

Airport/Ferry Area

The Victoria International Airport and the ferry landings at Swartz Bay and Sidney—all close together—are due north of Victoria about 7 miles (12 km), at the tip of the Saanich Peninsula. Sidney is the main town in the area, a pleasant small town with good shops, restaurants and lodging— and much lower rates than the Victoria area.

Hotel Sidney Waterfront Resort, 2537 Beacon Ave. (604-656-1131), has 44 units and a boat ramp where you can rent power or sailboats or go on charter fishing trips. Scuba diving equipment is also for rent. A restaurant and coffee shop are on the premises. *Inexpensive.*

Victoria Airport Travelodge, 2280 Beacon Ave. (604-656-1176), has 51 units and a heated pool. *Inexpensive.*

RV Parks

Paradise Retreat Centre & Campground, 2960 Irwin Rd., Victoria (604-478-6960), is on a 110-acre (44-ha) nature sanctuary, and is open May until September.

Island View Beach RV Camp, Homatco Rd., Saanichton (604-652-0548), is roughly halfway between Victoria and Sidney on the beach. Open May through September.

VICTORIA RESTAURANTS

Victoria's permanent population is smaller than the other two cities that make up the Evergreen Triangle, and the average tourist does not go there with fine food in mind. The ultra-British atmosphere, the boat and ferry rides to and from the city, the shops along Government Street are among the things that compete with restaurants for the tourist dollar. "British?" the average tourist says, "then let's have fish and chips."

In spite of this, Victoria does have some good places to eat, and only a scattering of them can be described as British. The Olde England Inn's Shakespeare Dining Room, noted earlier in the hotel section, is one. The Elephant and the Castle in the Eaton Centre at Government and View streets, which also serves steak and kidney pie, Cornish pasties and Old Country soups, is the other. And remember: Queen Victoria's full title was Queen Victoria, the Empress of India, so the city named in her honor also has some good East Indian restaurants.

Code: Inexpensive – Under $10 per person; Moderate – $10 to $30; Expensive – Over $30.

North American (a polite name for the U.S.)

Fuddruckers, 787 Hillside St. (604-386-4522), is where you'll find juicy burgers, grilled chicken breasts, grilled fish and all kinds of salads. *Inexpensive.*

Previous Pages:
*A marine vista from Vancouver
Island's driftwood-strewn shoreline.*
BRITISH COLUMBIA GOVERNMENT

Rattenbury's Restaurant, 703 Douglas St. (604-381-1333). This large restaurant in the very heart of the tourist area—it is part of the Crystal Gardens complex—is a good place to go if you don't want to make a production out of a meal but simply want something substantial to eat. Rattenbury's serves steaks, prime rib and seafoods, and sometimes salmon barbecue on the terrace. *Moderate.*

Blue Coyote Café, 1001 Wharf St. (604-382-1969), has a southwestern cuisine and decor. *Inexpensive.*

Chinese

Chinese Village Restaurant, 755 Finlayson St. (604-384-8151). This place, opposite Mayfair Shopping Centre, offers Cantonese, Szechuan and Mandarin. It also has a vegetarian menu. *Moderate.*

Ming's, 1321 Quadra St. (604-385-4405). Specializing in Szechuan and vegetarian dishes, Ming's was once voted the best Chinese restaurant in Victoria. Home delivery is offered if you have a hunger for Chinese and don't want to go out. *Moderate.*

East Indian

Da Tandoor, 1010 Fort St. (604-383-8332), is one of the city's most popular restaurants. Specializing in northern Indian food, all meats and breads are baked in a red-clay oven imported from Pakistan. Poultry, lamb, vegetarian dishes and seafood are served with the firepower of the spices chosen by each diner. *Inexpensive.*

Taj Mahal Restaurant, 679 Herald St. (604-383-4662), is another popular restaurant with a similar Tandoori menu and food baked in a similar oven with charcoal. Specialties include Lamb Biryani, Beef Vindaloo and Prawn Masala. *Moderate.*

French

La Petite Columbe, 604 Broughton St. (604-383-3234). This small, intimate place in the downtown area is described as casually elegant. *Moderate.*

The Aerie, 600 Ebedora Lane, Malahat (604-743-7115). This restaurant isn't in downtown Victoria; it is perched on top of a mountain about 20 minutes' drive north of Victoria with views back to Victoria and beyond to the Olympic Mountains. Take the spectacle Lake turnoff along Malahat Highway. Several people say it is one of the best French restaurants on Vancouver Island, and definitely the most romantic. Many herbs are from the Aerie's own garden. *Expensive.*

Greek

Periklis, 531 Yates St. (604-386-3313). If you like belly dancing while you fill your own, try this place downtown on the weekend. If you don't like belly dancing (I've never especially liked the olive-oiled look myself), try it on another night. The food is good. Also serves lunch. *Moderate.*

Victoria's busy Inner Harbour. ∧
TOURISM BRITISH COLUMBIA

Pubs

As one would expect from a city that emulates England so closely, pubs are around almost every corner. There are so many on the island that a successful guidebook, *Island Pubbing,* has been in print for several years. Pubs are pleasant places to have lunch or a simple dinner, and are seldom as rowdy as taverns in other Canadian or American cities.

CULTURE

 Victoria has a lively cultural life, including a symphony, several other musical groups, wonderful museums and a large number of galleries. Granted, some of the places along Government Street that call themselves galleries for the tourist trade are little more than postcard and poster shops, but Victoria has a number of good galleries representing Canada's best artists.

Several Pacific Northwest Coast Indian artists show their carvings, paintings and masks in Victoria galleries. The famous Vancouver Island Cowichan sweaters, themselves an art form made by members of the Cowichan band, use only the natural colours of wool.

You can find Cowichan sweaters and other articles of clothing made by Cowichan band members at **Hill's Indian Crafts,** 1008 Government St. (604-385-3911). They are also sold at the **Cowichan Trading Ltd.,** 1328 Government St. (604-383,0321); **Canadiana Gifts and Souvenirs,** 1012 Government St. (604-384-3123); **Indian Craft Shoppe,** 905 Government St. (604-382-3643), and **Sasquatch Trading Ltd.,** 1233 Government St. (604-386-9033).

Galleries

Art Gallery of Greater Victoria, 1040 Moss St. (604-384-4101). Some the best historic and contemporary art in Victoria is housed here, making it one of the finest repositories of art in Canada. The collection includes a large collection of paintings by Emily Carr, British Columbia's most famous artist, as well as art from Europe, North America and Asia. Its Shinto shrine is on permanent display in the Japanese Garden and is the only entire such shrine outside Japan. Admission.

Arts of the Raven Gallery, 1015 Douglas St. (604-386-3731). The gallery represents contemporary Northwest Coast Indian and Inuit art. Tony Hunt, a master carver himself, is the director.

Beatrice Jumpsen Gallery, 208-1110 Government St. (604-380-0121). Several West Coast artists are represented in a variety of media. The gallery has frequent Wednesday Brown Bag lunches where you can meet the artist whose show is hanging at that time.

Gallery of the Arctic, 611 Fort St. (604-382-9012), handles Inuit sculpture and prints from Cape Dorset, Povungnituk, Pangnirtung and other Arctic villages.

Michelle Frost Gallery, 2188 Oak Bay Ave. (604-598-1344). This gallery specializes in Canadian contemporary art.

La Paz Raku Studio & Gallery, 16 Fan Tan Alley (604-383-5223). This is a combination art school for sculpture, pottery, drawing and raku, and also a gallery with exhibitions throughout the year.

Museums

Royal British Columbia Museum, 675 Belleville St. (604-387-3701). This is one of the great museums of North America, and quite unlike any others. Walk-through exhibits take you to the streets of a pioneer town with pies being baked in cabin kitchens. Nearby is a working Gold Rush waterwheel. You can board Captain Vancouver's ship *Discovery,* and enter a native longhouse. It is possible to walk to the bottom of the ocean, or you can stroll through a coastal rain forest or along a seashore. Exhibits focus on the natural and human history of British Columbia, and you will stand before a woolly mammoth, see deer in a forest, hear tweeting birds, and walk along a marsh. You can attend lectures, see films and participate in special event days.

The museum was founded in 1896 and housed in the Parliament Buildings across Government Street from 1898 to 1968, when it moved into its present quarters, specifically designed for museum activities. More than 10 million artifacts are stored in the anthropological, biological and historical collections, although only a fraction are on public display. Admission.

Thunderbird Park, behind the museum, displays a large collection of totem poles and includes a carving shed where artists are constantly at work creating new poles. Surrounding the museum is a garden with plants from all over British Columbia.

Royal London Wax Museum, 470 Belleville St. (604-388-4461). This unusual museum contains more than 200 life-size statues of famous figures in history and those in the news today. It also has a diorama of the Last Supper and a Chamber of Horrors. Admission.

Undersea Gardens, 490 Belleville St. (604-382-5717). Situated next door to the wax museum, visitors can stroll down a stairway with views through glass to the seabed. Scuba divers interact with fish and marine life, including an octopus. Admission.

Maritime Museum, 28 Bastion Square (604-385-4222). This museum is in the former Provincial Courthouse and tells the maritime story of British Columbia. Vessels include a dugout canoe that was sailed to England, and a 20-foot (6-m) ketch that was sailed solo around the world. Admission.

Stage Theatres

McPherson Playhouse Foundation, 3 Centennial Square (604-386-6121). This foundation manages the McPherson Playhouse and the Royal Theatre, which offer professional theater, opera, dance and rock concerts. The Royal Theatre is also home to the Victoria Symphony.

Kaleidoscope Playhouse, 520 Herald St. (604-475-4444), is the base for the new theatre group's 26-week season.

*Some visitors enjoy getting >
around Victoria's downtown
area via pedal power.*
TOURISM VICTORIA

Langham Court Theatre, 805 Langham Ct. (604-384-2142). Six plays are presented each year, each lasting two weeks.

Musical Organizations

Victoria Symphony, 846 Broughton St. (604-385-6515). The symphony has several programs that keep its musicians busy throughout much of the year. Among its offerings are Concerts for Kids, the Seagram Pops concerts, the Bach to Mozart series and a 20th Century Music series.

Pacific Opera Victoria, 1316 B Government St. (604-385-0222). This professional opera company offers three major operas each season.

The Civic Orchestra of Victoria, University of Victoria (604-658-4412), presents four concerts each year in the university's Centre Auditorium.

Nightlife

Victoria has about half a dozen established night clubs in the central part of town.

The Forge Cabaret, 919 Douglas St. (604-383-7137), has Top 40 rock and live music.

Harpo's Cabaret, 15 Bastion Sq. (604-385-5333), has live music and good views of the Inner Harbour.

Steamers Pub, 570 Yates St. (604-381-4340), specializes in rhythm and blues.

Sweetwater's Niteclub, #27 – 560 Johnson St. (604-383-7844), is for lovers of songs from the 70s onward. Dress code.

The Queen of Cumberland, >
*one of the smallest in the B.C.
Ferries fleet, operates between
Swartz Bay on Vancouver Island
and the outer Gulf Islands.*
B.C. FERRIES

It doesn't take long to drive from Victoria to Nanaimo: It is only 69 miles (111 km), and much of Highway 1 is four-lane. You can make it in an hour and a half. That is like saying you can "do" Vancouver in a morning or Seattle between lunch and 5:30 P.M. Slow down. Take your time. Smell the flowers and see the towns, take the back roads and make it a day trip.

A suggestion: If you are traveling by car and planning to see Butchart Gardens before heading north to Nanaimo, or if you just want to see the Saanich Peninsula, take Highway 17 to Sidney, switch over to the west side of the peninsula and follow the country roads south. You will pass picturesque farms and country schools, beautiful bays and thick forests. Drive back to Brentwood Bay near Butchart Gardens and catch the little ferry that runs from there northwest to **Mill Bay.** It is a pleasant half-hour ride, and if you get to the ferry landing early, you can walk around the village and have a sandwich or a drink at the Rusty Duck Marina Café, on a float below the ferry dock.

From the ferry landing, the country road follows the curvature of the shoreline and passes several B&Bs until it joins Highway 1 in Mill Bay. But you don't have to stay on the well-traveled route unless you want to. To get a feeling for the island, try the roads that turn back toward Satellite Channel, which separates Vancouver Island from Saltspring Island. You won't get lost because there aren't that many paved roads on the island and they all eventually commingle with Highway 1.

While the scenery east of Highway 1 down to the salt-water is mostly homes and small towns, to the west you will see some of British Columbia's most beautiful timberland. Environmental organizations have been fighting with the provincial government for decades to preserve as much old-growth timber as possible. There are two places in Canada where civility is checked at the door: One is on the floor of the Parliament, where the debates are laced with caustic commentary, and the other is in the environmental arena. Greenpeace was founded in Canada, mainly by British Columbians, and the struggle over how much of the Vancouver Island forests to cut has been particularly bitter.

For a look at the forest in question, drive west from Duncan on Highway 18 to Cowichan Lake and take any number of trails from the highway back into the forest. Here grow some of the tallest trees in Canada. Sitka spruces reach 230 feet (70 m), and one called the Carmanah Giant, believed to be the tallest tree in Canada, was recently measured at 313 feet (95 m).

The first town of real consequence beyond Mill Bay is **Duncan,** which has visitor attractions mixed in with its agricultural and logging economic base. Its billboards along Highway 1 call it the City of Totems because it has more than two dozen large, beautiful poles standing in public places. A dozen stand along the highway near the Information Centre, three are outside City Hall, five at the Court House complex and nine near the railway station. Most were carved by members of the local Cowichan band, but one, named "Te Awhio Whio" (The King of the Cedar Forest) was carved by a Maori from New Zealand named Rupari Te Whata who came to Duncan from the B.C. town's New Zealand sister city, Kaikohe. It stands at the fountain near City Hall.

To see the totems downtown, turn west off Highway 1 on Trunk Road to the railroad tracks, where the poles stand near the station. Turn right on Government Street just beyond the railroad and take it to the Court House complex. One of the poles here was believed to be the largest in diameter ever carved when it was completed in 1988. Carved from a cedar log donated by MacMillan Bloedel timber company, it stands 24 feet (7 m) tall and is 7 feet (2 m) in diameter.

The Native Heritage Centre, 200 Cowichan Way (604-746-8119), is a combination visitor attraction and educational center. You can watch canoes, totems, masks and various other traditional wooden artwork being carved. You can see traditional native ceremonies and dances performed and demonstrations of how the famous Cowichan sweaters are knitted. A six-course feast is served, followed by tribal dancing, with the audience encouraged to participate. A gift shop and art gallery display and sell products made at the Centre.

B.C. Forest Museum, (604-746-1251) just north of Duncan on Highway 1, is actually a park with a museum about forestry. The theme "Man in the Forest" covers every facet of activity from aboriginal times through to the present. The park's more than 100 acres (40 ha) of indoor and outdoor exhibits and walking trails detail the history of forestry in British Columbia. An original steam locomotive takes you from the entrance over a wooden-trestle bridge and through a farm to the main exhibits of a logging camp with operating milling equipment, such as a planer mill, blacksmith shop, and a working sawmill. Admission.

Continuing north, the next major town north is **Chemainus,** which has proven that if you paint murals on the sides of buildings, the tourists will come. Chemainus had a

sawmill that employed about 400 people, but in 1982 MacMillan Bloedel replaced it with an updated mill employing fewer than 200. This was a serious blow to the town, and put it on the edge of extinction. Then someone came up with the idea of painting the town's history. Artists were hired to paint murals on the sides of buildings that depicted incidents and people important to the town's past.

The plan worked. Not only did the tourists come, so did the awards; and copy-cat murals appeared in Washington towns, such as those on the Long Beach Peninsula, the eastern Washington town of Toppenish and others. The imitations are flattering to Chemainus and beneficial

One of a series of murals that attract ∨
visitors to Chemainus, Vancouver Island.
CHEMAINUS MURAL SOCIETY

because this small town—its citizens like to call it "The Little Town That Did"—gets credit for starting the craze.

Nearly half a million visitors pass through Chemainus each year, making the project a resounding success story. There are scenes depicting life in Chemainus before the European explorers arrived, scenes showing the first sailing ships, the sawmill industry, pioneer merchants, interiors of general stores, street scenes and so forth.

You are encouraged to park and stroll through town, following a set of yellow footprints that lead you on a self-guided tour including the museum. Shops line the streets and you can buy an ice cream cone, a T-shirt proclaiming that you are a Chemaniac, antiques or an expensive work of art. Down on the waterfront is a replica of a waterwheel of the kind that powered the first sawmill in 1862. You'll find several B&Bs in the Chemainus area. Stop in the Visitor Information Centre for a list and descriptions.

In spite of warnings to the contrary, if you are traveling in mid-week or off-season, it is sometimes more interesting to drive aimlessly through this area and select a place to stay by stumbling onto it. Many B&Bs have mushroomed along the side roads between Victoria and Nanaimo, and most will be more rewarding than an impersonal motel room. If you don't find lodging before dark, you can always drive to one of the towns and check into a motel.

(Some travelers make reservations to secure a room, then go in search of something better, and cancel the reservation, often at the very last minute. I find that despicable. Even if they cancel before the deadline, they may have cost the hotel that room and someone else from getting it. May they spend eternity sleeping in their car.)

The ferry to lightly populated Thetis and Kuper islands leaves from downtown Chemainus. **Kuper Island** is an Indian reserve and has no visitors' facilities. **Thetis Island** has a small marina and a park, and **Overbury Farm Resort** (604-246-9769) which features individual cabins.

NANAIMO

That's right: Those are real live palm trees you see as you drive into town. They are proof that Nanaimo is truly in the banana belt of Vancouver Island, and of British Columbia for that matter. Even more than Victoria's, Nanaimo's summers are normally warm and dry and the winters extremely mild. This sweet climate continues on across the Strait of Georgia to create the Sunshine Coast on the mainland between Horseshoe Bay and Lund.

Nanaimo was founded in the 1850s when rich veins of coal were found, and it has survived the demise of coal-fired steamships to become a major shipping port for wood products and fish. It is also the terminus for the major B.C. Ferry runs to the mainland at Horseshoe Bay, almost due east from town, and southeast to Tsawwassen. The balmy climate has made Nanaimo a popular place to retire or for Vancouverites to own a second home. This, plus the good boating and fishing, has caused Nanaimo to become the second largest city on the island with a population in excess of 50,000.

In addition to the calorie-heavy confection named for the town (see recipe for Nanaimo Bars on pages 182-83), Nanaimo is also famous throughout Canada and much of North America for one of the wackiest events in the region: the International Bathtub Race, held the third Sunday of July each year.

This ingenious competition is pure slapstick. It began in 1967 with 214 entries and only 14 completions. With that kind of success behind it, the race became an international event and now covers a week of equally wacky undertakings, including a Silly Boat Regatta.

The race itself is between one-man bathtubs mounted on flat boards each powered by an outboard motor no larger than 7.5 horsepower. It runs from Nanaimo's harbor to Vancouver's Kitsilano Beach, a 33.5-mile (54-km) run on the Strait of Georgia, which can be quite turbulent. The tubbers aren't in great danger because they are accompanied by a flotilla of power boats, and some of the tubs even complete the race.

Nobody loses. Competitors win a golden-coloured plug just for entering. There is also a trophy for finishing, another for being the first to sink, and so forth.

Sightseeing and Tours

The Nanaimo Tourist and Convention Bureau at 266 Bryden St. (604-754-8474) gives away brochures and maps. You can also sign on for guided tours here.

Malaspina College, 900 Fifth St. (604-753-3245), is worth a walk through because it sits high on a hill with great views across the Strait of Georgia, and its buildings are mostly made of cedar. It has an arboretum with a trail leading off into the forest. The **Tamagawa Gardens,** given to the school by its sister college in Tokyo, is another attraction.

Nanaimo Harbour. This workplace rivals Victoria's Inner Harbour in beauty and accessibility. Ships and tugs share

Nanaimo Bars

Nanaimo is a familiar name to candy lovers all over the world thanks to that wonderful concoction called the Nanaimo Bar. Nobody knows exactly when the scrumptious bars came into being. One version credits the Ladies Auxiliary of the Harewood Neighborhood Volunteer Fire Department. Another source says it was the ladies of the Anglican Church who invented it for a cookbook in 1936.

This is the recipe given out by the Nanaimo Chamber of Commerce.

Bottom Layer
125 mL (1/2 cup) butter
50 mL (1/4 cup) granulated sugar
75 mL (1/3 cup) unsweetened cocoa powder
1 tsp. vanilla
1 egg, beaten
500 mL (2 cups) graham cracker crumbs
250 mL (1 cup) shredded unsweetened coconut
125 mL (1/2 cup) chopped walnuts

space with ferries and pleasure craft and the waterfront is lined with a series of small parks:

Piper's Lagoon Park includes the **Centennial Museum,** situated on a hill with great views to the mainland. It has replicas of petroglyphs showing animals and humans, pioneer articles, and a large exhibit related to coal mining in the area. **Log Trophy Park** takes its straightforward name from its centerpiece, a trophy-sized log.

The Bastion, an oddly shaped tower, is all that remains of the Hudson's Bay Company fort, built in 1853. It now houses the **Hudson's Bay Company Museum.** During summer months, young men dressed in gunnery uniform march down to Bastion Street daily at noon to fire three cannons out toward the strait. Some say it is the only ceremonial cannon firing west of Ontario.

Place butter, sugar, cocoa, vanilla and egg into top of double boiler. Place over hot water; cook, stirring, until mixture is of custard consistency. Remove from heat and stir in graham cracker crumbs, coconut and nuts. Blend well. Pack mixture in buttered 2.5 L (9 ") square pan. Refrigerate at least 1 hour.

Filling
50 mL (1/4 cup) butter
25 mL (2 Tbsp.) milk
25 mL (2 Tbsp.) instant
    vanilla pudding powder
500 mL (2 cups)
    powdered sugar

Cream butter, blend milk and pudding powder and stir in. Add powdered sugar, mixing until smooth and creamy. Spread over cookie base. Refrigerate about 15 minutes, until firm.

Top Layer
2 squares semi-sweet
    chocolate
15 mL (1 Tbsp.) butter

Melt chocolate and butter. Spread over vanilla layer. Refrigerate until set. Before chocolate hardens completely, mark out squares. Makes about 24 squares.

Other Waterfront Attractions:

The Seaplane Terminal, which has a Victorian look, is near **Georgia Park** with its formal gardens and native canoes and totems. **Swy-a-lana Lagoon Park** is on a man-made tidal lagoon which serves as something of a sea garden with creatures living there by choice rather than because they are trapped there. Next is the **Maffeo-Sutton Park** with its picnic tables, playgrounds and tennis courts.

Actually, Nanaimo probably has more parks than any city its size in Canada; its citizens like to say it has more parks than people. **Piper's Lagoon Park** north of town is popular with windsurfers, as is **Departure Bay,** a beach that also attracts teenagers. **Bowen Park** is a short distance out of town. **Colliery Dam Park** has hiking trails around the lake behind the dam and good trout fishing. The list continues: **Planta Park, Sealand Park** and **Sugar Loaf Mountain Park.**

Bungy Jumping

South Sea Islanders invented diving from high places head first with a vine or cord to stop them at the last minute. New Zealanders altered the sport with long bungy cords, but Vancouver Islanders were the first to build a bridge especially for the sport. The **Bungy Jumping Bridge** (called the Bungy Zone), 8 miles (13 km) south of Nanaimo, was built 140 feet (42 m) above the Nanaimo River. People pay for the privilege of attaching a bungy cord to their ankles and jumping off the bridge. Information: 604-753-5867.

Nanaimo Hotels

Nanaimo is an enjoyable place for Vancouverites to get away for a weekend or a few days without having to spend a lot of time traveling. The city has attracted several good hotels and a wide selection of small resorts, motels and B&Bs.

The Coast Bastion Inn, 11 Bastion St. (800-663-1144 or 604-753-6601), is the city's largest with 179 rooms, each with a balcony and ocean views. It has a health club, a café, lounge and pub. *Expensive.*

Harbourview Days Inn, 809 Island Hwy. S. (604-754-8171), 1.2 miles (2 km) south of the downtown area, has 78 rooms, sauna, continental breakfast, views from some rooms, and a restaurant on the premises. *Moderate.*

Moby Dick Motel, 1000 Stewart Ave. (604-753-7111). This 45-unit motel is situated on the waterfront with good views of the ocean and harbor. Some of the large units have kitchens. *Inexpensive.*

Best Western Dorchester Hotel, 70 Church St. (604-754-6835). This recently redone hotel is in a historic building. Many of its 70 rooms have views across the Seaplane Terminal and the straits. It has a restaurant and cocktail lounge. *Moderate.*

Nanaimo Restaurants

The Grotto, 1511 Stewart Ave. (604-753-3303), probably Nanaimo's most popular restaurant, appears in virtually every guidebook. It serves just about everything: fresh seafood, steaks, burgers, salads, and is on the waterfront near the B.C. Ferries Terminal. *Inexpensive.*

Gina's Cafe, 47 Skinner St. (604-753-5411), another favorite that has the atmosphere of a small town café in a made-for-TV movie. Why that comparison? Recently its color scheme was blue and hot pink. Nothing sedate about this place, and the food is Tex-Mex by nationality. It sits on one of the most exciting pieces of property, at the edge of a cliff behind the Courthouse. *Inexpensive.*

Neighboring Islands

Three islands lie just offshore from Nanaimo—Newcastle, Protection and Gabriola—all part of the Nanaimo recreational complex.

Newcastle is more formally the **Newcastle Island Provincial Marine Park,** with several trails, picnic areas, boat moorage, campsites and lots of beaches. Only the caretakers live there, along with beaver, deer, rabbits, raccoons and lots of birds. A passenger ferry runs hourly from Maffeo-Sutton Park at the downtown quay during the summer.

Protection Island has a strange history. It once was connected to the mainland by a coal-mine shaft beneath the water. Some old-timers said that when they were working in the shaft they could hear the whistles of steamships passing overhead. The mine was closed in 1938. Now the island is mostly residential, and is reached by a passenger ferry.

Gabriola Island is the farthest north of the Gulf Islands and the largest of the three off Nanaimo. It has a population of about 2,500, many of whom are artists and craftspeople. You'll find several small resorts and B&Bs on the island, along with one of the more unusual rock formations along the coast. It is called the Malaspina Galleries, or the Galiano Galleries, and is a sandstone formation that looks like a huge wave coming toward you. The island also has some petroglyphs, good scuba diving beaches and lots of wildlife.

The car-passenger ferry to Gabriola Island from Nanaimo is a 20-minute ride and departs several times daily from the dock adjacent to the Harbour Shopping Centre. No passengers are taken on Wednesdays because that day is set aside for transporting dangerous cargo to and from the island.

A number of galleries and craft studios are scattered around the island. For information, call the Gabriola Chamber of Commerce (604-247-9332).

Recreation in the Evergreen Triangle

SKIING IN THE EVERGREEN TRIANGLE

Skiing is one of the major sports in the region, and the mountains that form the eastern boundary of this region are lined with ski resorts.

Beginning on the southern end of the triangle, **Snoqualmie Pass** is 53 miles (85 km) east of Seattle and has four major ski areas in a space of two miles: Alpental, Ski Acres, Snoqualmie, and Hyak. The average summit elevation is 5,400 feet (1645 m) and a base of 3,000 feet (900 m), for a vertical drop of 2,200 feet (670 m). The four have 25 chair lifts among them, and 11 rope tows. Snowboarders are welcome only at Ski Acres and Snoqualmie. All have ski shops, day lodges, food service, and bus service to the area. For bus reservations to all areas call 360-232-8162. Snow conditions for all four: 360-976-7623. Some condominium rentals are available (the information numbers above can give details) and the Best Western Summit Inn (1-800-528-1234) has overnight lodging. RV parking is permitted in the summit parking lots, but no hookups are available.

Stevens Pass (360-973-2441) is 80 miles (128 km) east of Seattle on US Highway 2 and has an elevation of 3,800 to 5,800 feet (1150 to 1765 m) with a vertical drop of 1,800 feet (550 m). It has 36 runs, 15 lifts, one quad, 6 doubles, 4 triples, 4 rope tows, child care, schools, shop, rentals, restaurant, and cafeteria.

Mount Baker (360-734-6771) is 56 miles (90 km) east of Bellingham on Route 542. It has an elevation range from 3,500 to 5,040 feet (1060 to 1535 m) and a vertical drop of 2,200 feet (670 m). It has 38 runs, 9 lifts, 6 double chairs, 2 quads, a rope tow, a day lodge, child care and food services.

The Vancouver area has the most spectacular skiing in the region. It is one of the few cities in North America with ski runs that offer views of the city. At night Grouse Mountain is visible from the downtown area and the other ski areas are only slightly less accessible.

Grouse Mountain (604-984-0661) is due north of Vancouver and reached by driving up Nancy Greene Way in North Vancouver. You can also take public transportation to the mountain's base, where the 50-passenger Skyride aerial tram runs to the 3,700-foot (1127-m) summit. The mountain has 13 runs with 4 double chairs, 2 T-bars, 3 rope tows and a handle tow.

Mount Seymour (604-986-2261) is about half an hour's drive to the east on Mount Seymour Parkway and is known for its easier slopes and cross-country skiing and snowshoeing. Snowboarding is also popular. It caters more to families and is said to have the busiest ski school and rental shop in Western Canada. Seymour has 25 runs with 4 double chairs and a rope tow.

To the west is **Cypress Bowl** (206-926-6007), reached by a road leading off Upper Levels Highway above West Vancouver. Cypress is known for its two-mile run from Mount Strachan with views of Howe Sound. It has 25 runs with 4 double chairs. Nearby Hollyburn Ridge has 10 miles (16 km) of cross-country trails.

The biggest resort of them all is 75 miles (120 km) north of the Evergreen Triangle, but an important part of the region's recreation. The Whistler-Blackcomb complex is almost a complete city that operates the year around.

Whistler Mountain (604-687-6761) has 85 ski runs with two new high-speed chairs that take only 15 minutes to reach the top of the 5,020-foot (1530-m) peak. It also has four-person gondolas, a ten-person gondola, 2 T-bars, 2 tows, 7 double chairlifts and 4 triple chairlifts. One of Whistler's most popular runs is the Olympic which takes skiers from the mountain down into Whistler Village.

Blackcomb Mountain (604-687-7507) is adjacent to Whistler and has a quad car called the Glacier Express that takes skiers onto Blackcomb Glacier. Blackcomb's Mile High run is 5,280 feet (1609 m), slightly higher than Whistler.

The largest ski area on Vancouver Island is **Mount Washington** (604-338-1386), north of Nanaimo near Comox. It has 5 lifts (1 quad, 2 triple and 2 double chairlifts) to 44 runs, and a Nordic ski area with some 19 miles (30 km) of groomed trails.

While skiing at these resorts, you may want to pick up brochures on their summer programs. Most have found ways to capitalize on summer recreation, such as using the chair lifts to take hikers and mountain bikers into the back-country, and to make use of the condominiums and lodges for conferences.

SCUBA DIVING IN THE EVERGREEN TRIANGLE

British Columbia has a mainland coastline 4,350 miles (7000 km) long and if you count the coastlines of the hundreds of islands of all sizes the total would be about double. Washington has more than 2,400 miles (3900 km) of coastline and all this adds up to some of the most varied and spectacular cold-water diving in the world.

Sport divers can arm-wrestle with a playful octopus, scratch the chin of a 6-foot (2-m) wolf-eel or explore the remains of a century-old shipwreck. Invertebrates are among the most intriguing animals to be seen, with nearly 30 species of seastars in shallow water, several dozen species of nudibranchs, graceful anemones up to 3 feet (1 m) tall, towering sea whips over 6 feet (2 m) tall and giant Pacific octopuses that tip the scales at over 100 lbs. (45 kg).

While the fish generally lack the bizarre patterns and colors of their tropical counterparts, there are notable exceptions, such as the Red Irish Lord sculpin, decorated warbonnet, and several dozen species of strikingly marked rockfish. Large marine mammals are also found, including northern sea lions, which can exceed 1,100 lbs. (500 kg). Here, too, killer whales roam the coast in distinct family pods.

Winters are mild and that's when some of the best diving takes place. Plankton levels and freshwater run-off are at their lowest during the winter months, resulting in remarkably transparent water. In the clearest regions, underwater visibility can reach 100 feet (30 m), creating superb conditions for underwater photographers and video enthusiasts. During spring and summer, plankton bloom and run-off combine to make water clarity unpredictable. Often, however, it's only the shallow, uppermost layer that is clouded;

clear water usually underlies the warmer, less saline surface water.

A high-quality wetsuit or drysuit is a necessity for diving comfortably summer or winter. Water temperatures drop to about 45° to 50° Fahrenheit (10°C) in the winter. In the summer, the surface layer warms considerably to 60° Fahrenheit (15°C), but below the thermocline, temperatures rarely exceed 50° Fahrenheit (10°C), requiring a complete suit with hood, boots and gloves.

Recreational diving is a thriving service industry on both sides of the international boundary with professional dive stores, resorts, charter boat operations and suit manufacturers. Virtually anything a traveling diver might require, from guided dive trips to repair of a troublesome regulator, can be found. Some resorts cater especially to divers, providing package group rates that include boat charters, gear washdown, storage lockers and film processing.

Where to Dive

Victoria

Tidal currents flowing past Victoria are quite swift, resulting in rich marine life. Several excellent shore dive sites are found near Victoria, including Saxe Point Park, the Ogden Point Breakwater, Ten-mile Point and Willis Point for deep diving.

According to Tourism B.C., the most exciting dive site in the Victoria area is Race Rocks, 11 miles (18 km) southwest of Victoria harbor, which has striking scenery both above and below the water. Here divers can swim with northern sea lions, male California sea lions and harbor seals.

Below the surface, strong currents sweep between the rugged islets, carrying plankton to a lush growth of invertebrates. The bottom is alive with colorful life: purple and red hydrocorals, ghostly white plumose anemones; purple, green, orange and red brooking anemones and graceful basketstars extending their many-branched arms into the current's flow.

Several professional dive shops in Victoria provide equipment sales, service, rentals and instruction. Many also offer guided charter services, and some resorts offer all-inclusive dive packages.

Sidney

Sidney lies on the eastern shore of Saanich Peninsula facing Haro Strait where numerous islands dot the landscape and the broken rock sea floor has gardens of brilliant orange sea cucumbers, gaudy nudibranchs, hydroids and pinto abalone.

Saanich Inlet is a sheltered area where you can dive when Haro Strait is too rough. The inlet has giant cloud-sponge formations below 80 feet (24 m) and features exceptional water clarity in the winter.

The southern Gulf Islands, including Saltspring, Mayne, North and South Pender and Galiano, can be reached by ferry or charter boat from Sidney and have resorts that offer accommodations, a number with compressed air for dive tanks.

Nanaimo

Nanaimo is the Vancouver Island terminus of one of the principal ferry routes from the mainland. Only an hour and 45 minutes from Vancouver, it is situated near the northern Gulf Islands where there are several excellent dive sites in current-swept passages such as Dodd Narrows, Gabriola Passage and Porlier Pass. During the late winter, thousands of sea lions, eagles and cormorants congregate in nearby Northumberland Channel to gorge on schools of herring.

The best known diving area is 4 Fathom Reef where enormous octopi and wolf eel are found. The destroyer *Chaudière* was sunk there, making it the world's largest artificial reef.

Courtenay

Two large islands, Denman and Hornby, off eastern Vancouver Island just south of Courtenay, are popular destinations. Hornby especially has gained fame as a location where 12-foot (4-m) six-gill sharks can be seen on the deep reefs. Shipwrecks can also be found here, including the *Alpha*, a 220-foot (67-m) iron steamer which ran aground on Chrome Island at the southern tip of Denman in 1900.

Vancouver

Several full-service dive stores can be found in Vancouver and day-trip and weekend dive charters are available to the Gulf Islands, about 25 miles (40 km) across the Strait of Georgia. From Vancouver, divers also can make connections and charter arrangements for destinations north along the mainland coast and Vancouver Island.

Puget Sound

San Juan Islands

Some of the best diving in Washington is in the San Juan Islands, especially on the west and north coast of San Juan Island. Reuben Tarte Cove on the northeast end of the island has large rocks and ledges that provide shelter for a variety of fish. San Juan County Park, on the west side of the island, is another popular diving area. It has four entry points with a choice of sandy to rocky bottoms. Lime Kiln Point State Park on the northwest side is one of the most popular because of the combination of bull kelp that forms a cover and the series of ledges and walls that attract a large variety of sea life.

Orcas and Lopez islands have good sites as well. Brown Rock is on the very tip of the eastern arm of Orcas Island and is perhaps the best place to dive on the large island, at least in terms of the sea life found there. Of the three or four sites on Lopez Island, Agate Beach County Park has the most beautiful setting. It is situated in a rocky cove with Johns Point on the north and Iceberg Point on the south. The bay is relatively shallow with lots of sea grass and a wide selection of animals.

Another popular area is along the shores of Admiralty Inlet, where Puget Sound and the Strait of Juan de Fuca meet. Fort Worden and Fort Flagler state parks on the Kitsap Peninsula, and Fort Casey on Whidbey Island all offer good diving.

Whidbey Island

Another prime diving area. Rosario Beach is a short distance north of Deception Pass State Park where you will find rock formations, several colors of sea urchins, hermit crabs, sea cucumbers, nudibranches, stars, chitons and several species of fish.

Edmonds

The small town of Edmonds has Puget Sound's first underwater park, adjacent to the Edmonds-Kingston ferry landing. The park was created by sinking an old drydock and parts of boats, then adding an underwater "trail" for divers to follow. As with many diving areas with platforms, divers have to share them from time to time with sea lions, who tend to become territorial and quite aggressive.

Check with local dive shops for more information, regulations and diving groups to join for outings.

GOLFING IN THE EVERGREEN TRIANGLE

Thanks to the usually benign climate, golfing is a popular year-round sport and there's an abundance of courses throughout the region. Here is a sampling of public courses.

Washington

Anacortes: Similk Beach Golf Course, 1250 Christianson Rd. (360-293-5355), 18 holes.

Bellingham: Action Golf, 1066 Lakeway (206-676-5766), 9 holes. Lake Padden Golf Course, 4882 Samish Wy. (360-676-6989), 18 holes.

Blaine: Semiahmoo Golf Course, 8720 Semiahmoo Wy. (360-371-7005), 18 holes. Sea Links Golf Course, 7878 Birch Bay Dr. (360-371-7933), 18 holes.

Custer: Grandview Golf Course, 7738 Portal Wy. (360-366-3947), 18 holes.

Everett: Harbor Pointe Golf Course, 11817 Harbor Pt. Blvd. (206-355-6060), 18 holes.

Ferndale: Riverside Golf Course, 5799 Riverside Dr. (360-384-4116), 9 holes.

Mount Vernon: Overlook Golf Course, 1785 State Hwy. 9 (360-422-6444), 9 holes.

Port Angeles: Peninsula Golf Club, 105 Lindberg Rd. (360-457-6501), 18 holes.

Port Townsend: Port Townsend Golf Club, 1948 Blaine St. (360-385-072), 9 holes.

Seattle: Jackson Park Golf Course, 1000 N.E. 135th St. (206-363-4747, 18 holes. Jefferson Park Golf Course, 4101 Beacon Ave. S. (206-762-4513), 18 holes.

British Columbia

Vancouver: Fraserview Golf Course, 7800 Vivian Dr. (604-280-8633), 18 holes. University Golf Club, 5185 University Blvd. (604-224-1818), 18 holes. McCleery Golf Course, 7170 Macdonald St. (604-261-4524), 18 holes.

West Vancouver: Gleneagles Golf Course, 6190 Marine Dr. (604-921-7353), 9 holes.

Richmond: Greenacres Golf Course, 5040 No. 6 Rd. (604-273-1121), 18 holes.

Surrey: Peace Portal Golf Course, 16900 4th Ave. (604-538-4818), 18 holes.

Victoria: Cedar Hill Municipal Golf Course, 1400 Derby Rd. (604-595-3103), 18 holes. Cordova Bay Golf Course, 5333 Cordova Bay Rd. (604-658-4075), 18 holes. Olympic View Golf Course, 643 Latoria Rd. (604-474-3673), 18 holes. Prospect Lake Golf Course, 4633 Prospect Lake Rd. (604-479-2688), 9 holes. Royal Oak Inn Golf Course, 540 Marsett Pl. (604-658-1443), 9 holes.

Duncan: Duncan Lakes Golf & Country Club, Hwy. 18 and North Rd. (604-746-6789), 18 holes.

Qualicum Beach: Eaglecrest Golf Course, 2035 Island Hwy. W. (604-752-9744), 18 holes.

Sidney: Glen Meadows Golf and Country Club, 1050 McTavish Rd. (604-656-3136), 18 holes.

Tourist Information

Washington

Bellevue
East King County Convention
& Visitors Bureau
520 – 112th Ave. N.E.,
Suite 101
Bellevue, WA 98004
(206-455-1926)

Bellingham
Bellingham/Whatcom County
Visitors & Convention
Bureau
904 Potter St.
Bellingham, WA 98227
(360-671-3990)
(1-800-487-2032)

Blaine
Blaine Visitor
Information Center
900 Peace Portal Dr.
Blaine, WA 98230
(360-332-4544)

Edmonds
Edmonds Visitors Bureau
120 Fifth Ave. N.
Edmonds, WA 98020
(206-778-6711)

La Conner
La Conner Chamber
of Commerce
Lime Dock Building
La Conner, WA 98257
(360-466-4778)

Langley
Langley Chamber
of Commerce
124½ Second St.
Langley, WA 98260
(360-221-6765)

Lynden
Lynden Chamber
of Commerce
1775 Front St.
Lynden, WA 98264
(360-354-5995)

Oak Harbor
North Whidbey Chamber
of Commerce
5506 S.R. 20
Oak Harbor, WA 98277
(360-675-3535)

Port Angeles
Port Angeles Chamber
of Commerce
121 Railroad Ave.
Port Angeles, WA 98362
(360-452-2363)

Port Townsend
Port Townsend Chamber
of Commerce
2437 Sims Way
Port Townsend, WA 98368
(360-385-2722)

San Juan Islands
San Juan Islands
Tourism Cooperative
P.O. Box 65
Lopez, WA 98261
(360-468-3663)

Seattle
Seattle/King County
Convention & Visitors
Bureau
800 Convention Pl.,
Eighth Ave. & Pike St.
Seattle, WA 98101
(206-461-5840)

Sequim
Sequim Visitor
Information Center
1192 E. Washington St.
Sequim, WA 98382
(360-683-6197)

Washington State Ferries
Colman Dock
Seattle, WA 98104
(206-464-6400)

**Washington Department
of Trade & Economic
Development**
Tourism Development
Division
P.O. Box 42500
Olympia, WA 98504-2500
(206-586-2088)

British Columbia

B.C. Ferry Corporation
1112 Fort St.
Victoria, B.C. V8V 4V2
Victoria (604-656-0757)
Vancouver (604-685-1021)
Nanaimo (604-753-6626)

**British Columbia
Development**
Ministry of Tourism
865 Hornby St. #802
Vancouver, B.C. V6Z 2G3
(604-660-2861)

**Duncan-Cowichan Chamber
of Commerce**
381 Trans Canada Highway
Duncan, B.C. V9L 3R5
(604-746-4421)

**Ladysmith Chamber
of Commerce**
PO Box 598
Ladysmith, B.C. V0R 2E0
(604-245-2112)

**Nanaimo Tourist &
Convention Bureau**
266 Bryden St.
Nanaimo, B.C. V9S 1A8
(604-754-8474)

**Saanich Peninsula
Chamber of Commerce**
P.O. Box 2014
Sidney, B.C. V8L 3S3
(604-656-0525)

**Tourism Association
of Southwestern B.C.**
#304 – 828 West 8th Ave.
Vancouver, B.C. V5Z 1E2
(604-876-8916)

Tourism Vancouver
Waterfront Centre,
Suite 210 – 200 Burrard St.
Vancouver, B.C. V6C 3L6
(604-682-2222)

**Tourism Association
of Vancouver Island**
#302 – 45 Bastion Sq.
Victoria, B.C. V8W 1J1
(604-382-3551)

Tourism Victoria
812 Wharf St.
Victoria, B.C. V8W 1T3
(604-382-2127)

Bibliography

B.C. Historical Association, Gulf Islands Branch.
A Gulf Islands Patchwork. Victoria: 1961.

Baker, Carol. *Essential Vancouver and British
Columbia*. London, England: The Automobile
Association, 1991.

Coo, Bill. *Scenic Rail Guide to Western Canada*.
Toronto: Greey de Pencier, 1985.

Cummings, Al, and Jo Bailey. *Gunkholing in the San
Juans*. Edmonds, WA: Nor'Westing. n.d.
—*Gunkholing in the Gulf Islands*. Edmonds, WA:
Nor'Westing, 1986.

Elliott, Marie. *Mayne Island & The Outer Gulf
Islands*. Mayne Island, B.C.: Gulf Islands Press, 1984.

Fischnaller, Stephen. *Northwest Shore Dives*.
Olympia, WA: Bio-Marine Images, 1993.

Fraser, Marian Botsford. *Walking the Line: Travels
Along the Canadian/American Border*. San Francisco:
Sierra Club Books; Vancouver: Douglas & McIntyre,
1989.

Gerber, Anne, with Lorraine Gannon. *The Serious
Shopper's Guide To Vancouver and Beyond*.
Vancouver: Serious Publishing, 1992.

King, Jane. *British Columbia Handbook*. Chico, CA:
Moon Publications, 1989.

Maikle, Dene S., editor. *The Complete Victoria
Handbook*. Victoria: Victoria Information Services,
1986.

Nanton, Isabel and Mary Simpson. *Adventuring in
British Columbia*.Vancouver: Douglas & McIntyre,
1991.

OBEE, BRUCE. *The Gulf Islands*. North Vancouver: Gray's/Whitecap, 1981.

RICHARDSON, DAVID. *Pig War Islands*. Eastsound, WA: Orcas Publishing Company, 1971.

SCOTT, JAMES W. and MELLY A. REULING. *Washington Public Shore Guide: Marine Waters*. Seattle: University of Washington Press, 1986.

THOMAS, CAROLYN and JILL STEWART. *Island Treasures: 2*. Madeira Park, B.C.: Harbour Publishing, 1990.

WERSHLER, TERRI. *The Vancouver Guide*. Vancouver: Douglas & McIntyre, 1993.

Index

Notes

Notes

Notes

Notes

Notes

Notes

Notes

Notes